ALSO BY CHARLES FORAN:

FICTION

Kitchen Music

Butterfly Lovers

House on Fire

Carolan's Farewell

NON-FICTION

Sketches in Winter

The Last House of Ulster

The Story of My Life (so far)

JOIN THE REVOLUTION, COMRADE

Journeys And Essays

JOIN · THE REVOLUTION, COMRADE

JOURNEYS · AND · ESSAYS

CHARLES FORAN

BIBLIOASIS

FIRST EDITION

Library and Archives Canada Cataloguing in Publication

Foran, Charles, 1960-
    Join the revolution, comrade : journeys and essays / Charles Foran.

ISBN 13: 978-1-897231-41-8
ISBN 10: 1-897231-41-5

    I. Title.

PS8561.O633J63 2008   c814'.54   C2008-900199-0

Edited by Daniel Wells

 Canada Council   Conseil des Arts
for the Arts   du Canada

 ONTARIO ARTS COUNCIL
CONSEIL DES ARTS DE L'ONTARIO

We gratefully acknowledge the support of the Canada Council for the
Arts and the Ontario Arts Council for our publishing program.

PRINTED AND BOUND IN CANADA

In memory of Elizabeth Bierk, 1954-2006

CONTENTS

BOOKS

PREFACE

All men's miseries, Pascal observed, derive from not being able to sit in a quiet room alone. The aphorism, composed, no doubt, in a quiet room alone, smacks of writerly unease and claustrophobia, cleverly posited as its inverse. Confined to his desk every day, the occasional bored cat or window-sill bird as passing company, the author must therefore be the most happy of women or men? Seated in his chair week after week, year upon year, while people scurry by outside, generally in one another's arms?

To express the anxiety differently, a novelist friend tells an anecdote about turning forty. The friend visited his parents on the auspicious date. His father, a retired machinist, sat down with his boy for some celebratory drinking. Once sufficiently lubricated, the father confessed a question he had been too embarrassed to ask for ages. "Your mother and I are proud of your accomplishments, son," he said. "Very proud. But what exactly do you *do* for a living?"

I first intended to title this collection after one of my own father's favourite expressions, also the name of a piece about growing up in Southern Ontario. "Dumb as a Sack of Hammers" certainly has a ring to it. The word 'dumb' especially, once permitted both its literal and slang meanings, seems note perfect; 'dumb' as in less-than-intellectually-robust, and 'dumb' as in lacking the powers of speech. Wordsmiths they may be, writers can easily pass entire working days without saying a thing. This is not a judgement of their prose. It is an observation about their mouths, which aren't often required to open. Email has supplanted the phone in most business exchanges. Spouses or lovers wisely wait until dinner before resuming contact. Those sill birds are willing, but speak in strange tongues. Cats could care less about the loneliness of others.

On one level, this is how it should be. Writers, point of fact, talk all the time while in their rooms. They've loads to say about every manner of subject. Try hushing them up about a few nagging concerns. The chatter is voluble and incessant and can be tiresome. But unless there is a problem in the head, it is never a monologue. Regardless of the form – novel or poem, essay or play – this is a conversation. At its best, it is an ongoing one, and it is between you and me. Directly. Without interruption.

Two thirds of these pieces are devoted to the classic subjects of literary conversations. Words and books represent in equal parts the implements of the trade, and the tradition backing it. Writing essays about words or about other books may strike some as boring insider stuff. For certain hardliners, though, writing is only about language and literature is only concerned with other literature. That view is too narrow, not to mention death to conversations, but the truth remains that prose is indeed made of words and books are first, if not foremost, negotiating with other books. In short, such concerns aren't shop talk; they *are* the shop, along with the building the shop is in and the surrounding block of properties.

Still, the title I have chosen captures my own feelings of claustrophobia after sitting alone all day, and the life – and career, by default – choices that have resulted. *Join the Revolution, Comrade* is, fittingly, a line spoken by another friend, and a lift from a movie. In 1983, a young Beijing teacher named Zhou Shuren was given a brief part in Bernardo Bertolucci's *The Last Emperor*, then being shot in the capital. In his scene Zhou played a Red Guard. Marching in a rally, he counsels a curious bystander – the former emperor of China, no less – to abandon his bourgeois tendencies, and be quick about it. Scriptwriters apparently struggled with the line he would speak. Different versions were considered.

1. "Join our glorious revolution, friend, or go screw yourself and your family."
2. "Help fight against the Liu Shaoqi clique, comrade, or else be a running dog."
3. "Support the Great Helmsman, brother, or I'll smash your face in."

Version #1, it was felt, suffered from an excess of 'f' sounds; #2 was deemed obscure, especially the wonky reference to greyhounds. The third epithet, while nicely menacing, sounded too loud a note of individual initiative ("*I'll* smash your face in"), inappropriate in a workers' paradise. The winning line, in contrast, captured all the sensitivity and egalitarianism of a Red Guard sallying forth to abuse and denigrate for the glory of Mao. "Join the revolution, Comrade," Zhou duly hissed into the camera, "or else fuck off."

By the time I met Zhou Shuren four years later, the line had morphed into a mantra of ironic detachment from his own life and career. "Join the revolution, Comrade," he would advise any and everyone, regardless of the topic. Sometimes Zhou delivered the kicker, eyes glinting with mischief and beer, but on most occasions he allowed the sentence to trail off, an implied entreaty or insult or, more often, a non sequitur worthy of Ionesco.

Others probably heard despair and alcohol in the mantra, and dismissed it accordingly. But I, detecting both rebuke and challenge, took the advice seriously. How I tried to join that revolution is explored in the essay bearing that name. It is a tale of friendship and failure, and it anchors the third of the text devoted to being out of Pascal's chamber and amongst those with the open arms. In this instance, the arms are Asian, a corner of the world that continues to preoccupy my dreams, waking and otherwise.

Whether in the room or in the world, however, the standard remains the same. "All writing," Martin Amis says, "is a campaign against cliché. Not just clichés of the pen but clichés of the mind and clichés of the heart." I keep this dictum on a wall next to my computer, and glance at it every morning. Mostly, I do so in annoyance and pouty resentment. The measure is impossible. No one has the time or, face it, originality to be so vigilant. The notion of participating in such a campaign alone could well produce a brain aneurism. Whose fault would that be? More galling still, Amis throws down this gauntlet at the outset of a collection of literary journalism, *The War Against Cliché*, that is incisive, excoriating and funny – not to mention devoid of bromides of any sort, including those invoking the ritual tossing of a glove as challenge. His fiction, small mercies, does contain the occasional cliché, usually originating from the chest region, though certainly not the wicked aneurism motif that runs through *The Information*.

But he is right about writing; to be good it must be, however quietly, fresh of thought and perception. It must be this way on each page of the novel that took a decade to complete and, equally, in every paragraph of the travel piece composed in a hotel room or the profile written up over a weekend. There is no shirking this revolution, either. There is no lying to the pen-and-page or computer screen. The possibilities of language are the same, as are the stakes.

PLACES

JOIN THE REVOLUTION, COMRADE:

My June 4th Obsession

I

I am always more distressed and worried by the death of a friend or student if I did not know when, where, or how he died. And I imagine that from their point of view to perish at the hands of a few butchers in a dark room is more bitter than dying in public.

—Lu Xun

Shu Sheyu had a bum leg, courtesy of childhood polio. He taught classics at the college. On campus, Shu was known to colleagues and students equally as 'the cripple'. His face resembled an opera mask: a high forehead, arcing dark brows and distended dark eyes, smooth wide cheeks and thick lips. He wasn't only curious, contrary and bright. Indifferent to opinions of him – a skin toughened during that same childhood – and flaunting of rules, posted or otherwise, Shu Sheyu was also extravagant in his appetites and opinions. He delighted in excesses of food and drink. In measured, thoughtful English, he mused on the deep structures of Chinese culture, prejudice by prejudice, cruelty by cruelty. He could certainly speak to the cruelties. Ever alert for his queue in the theatre of the absurd that he saw as his own life, Shu participated in an inter-department track meet one afternoon. The various departments made a ceremonial turn of the grounds at the outset. Shu limped along with the history crew, holding a sign that described his team as: AN OLD MAN, A WOMAN, AND THE CRIPPLE. He insisted on not just running the relay race but claiming the final position. Nearing the finish line thirty seconds behind the rest of the heat, his bad leg splayed at a forty-five degree angle, Shu broke into a grin. Turning to the bleachers, he offered the crowd a flawless imitation of a champion

17

leaning into the tape, chest thrust out and baton raised, features wrenched in joyous agony.

As Shu declined to take an English name, everyone, Chinese and foreigners alike, just called him Shu. He was a bracing presence at parties and dinners.

Zhang Naiying, in contrast, preferred that we call her Francis. She became friends with my wife. A native Beijinger who had studied at the college a few years before, Francis was an attractive woman with a frank, friendly smile. Her face kept no secrets; when sad she looked crestfallen; when happy she lit like a flattered diva. Her youth, appearance, and membership in the Communist Party – an exclusive club with twenty million members, all but a handful now disinterested in either paying dues or attending functions – elevated her star in the English department. Students adored her and men sought her companionship. Francis flaunted her status less for romance or promotion than to allow her to find better-paying work as a tour guide and translator, while still keeping her campus apartment and pay packet, along with the ration tickets that allowed for purchases of rice, wheat and meat. An entrepreneur at heart, she had some patience for academia but none for her male colleagues, whom she found meek and feckless, emasculated, perhaps, by politics.

Once, at a dinner in our apartment, Shu Sheyu divided a plate of tortillas I had made into four portions. "The Four Modernizations," Shu called them, referring to the government campaign to encourage advancement in key sectors. Francis watched as the men at the table devoured Industry, Agriculture, Science and Technology, and National Defence. When I inquired about the phantom "Fifth Modernization" – the phrase coined a decade earlier by imprisoned dissident Wei Jingsheng to include democracy and human rights – Zhang Naiying raised an eyebrow in scepticism and, I sensed, disapproval at my own sally into the dangerous waters of political wit.

Men, her expression inferred – fools for generalities and abstractions. Fools for ideas that bring only grief.

Ding Luojin, too, had no time for ideas. Actually, Luojin, a third-year student with oversized glasses and Cultural Revolution pigtails that she chewed on while she spoke, had no time for anything, except our apartment, and reading novels. The allure of the apartment was obvious: a stocked kitchen, a sitting room with couches and a TV, space heaters in all three rooms. Classrooms, on the other hand, were unheated and students were careful to probe the cafeteria rice with their chopsticks, searching for pebbles or cockroaches. Dormitories, meanwhile, offered only the warmth generated by six undergraduates sharing each pinched, whitewashed cell, with toilets located at the end of unlit hallways. Besides visiting us, Luojin's favourite pastime was reading under her coverlet in her bunk. Being a pupil of English, it might be expected she would concentrate on western novels. She did, but not in their language of origin. In this bias, she was far from singular. Once I queried students about their summer reading lists, books meant to be read in the original. One young man claimed he had devoured the works of Ernest Hemingway over the holidays. When I asked for titles, he stumbled translating the too-literal Chinese titles back into English: *The Old Man and his Fish* and *Goodbye, Arm*. Another undergraduate boasted of having made it through all 500 pages of John Steinbeck's masterpiece in its incantatory American. And the title of that masterpiece? *"The Angry Grapes,"* the student replied after a struggle.

But Ding Luojin struggled hardly at all. Her love of English novels, and her desire to learn English well enough to evade her government-ordained destiny to be returned to her hometown in central China and assume duties as a tour guide in a region devoid of tourists, could not match her need to be consoled by reading about other worlds in the language of her own. The longer those English-novels-in-Chinese, she explained to us after a rapturous plot summary of *Gone with the Wind*, the better. "What else do you read?" I asked her once. "Nothing else," she answered in her whispery voice. "Only long novels. Many days we all stay in our beds and read. It is better than going outside." "Outside the campus?" my wife said. "Outside the room," Luojin clarified. "All six of you in the room, all day?" I said. "We forget together," she replied, chewing on hair.

Mind you, Zhou Shuren, my closest friend in Beijing the winter and spring of 1988-89, sought to conduct his life within an even wider shadow of forgetfulness. Zhou, who had accepted an American teacher's suggestion of the English moniker 'Julius,' taught English grammar and film studies at the college. His nature, though, was that of an artist, albeit one as yet undiscovered by his medium. Off-campus, he hung out with painters and musicians, including Cui Jian, the avatar of Chinese rock and roll. He also kept company with the city's hoodlum underclass, known as *liu-meng*, a loose confederation of punks and petty criminals, nihilists and existential heroes whose reputation derived from their habits of smoking and drinking to bellicose, belching extremity in grotty bars, as well as buzzing around the dimly-lit imperial boulevards at night on motorcycles. On-campus, Zhou struck a purposefully pre-grunge grunge pose. Bangs of greasy hair fell over his fine-boned face, shading an often bleary gaze and cheeks that showed in their opened pores the ravages of too little sleep and far too much alcohol. He wore a goatee, wispy and apologetic, and his teeth were neither white nor aligned, especially the lower shelf. Shabby T-shirts and torn pants were his favoured apparel, in classroom or out, and he was exceedingly pleased to be the latest owner of a pair of army boots, their laces gone missing.

Beer was one path to forgetting. I kept our kitchen bar fridge stocked for Zhou's visits, which could occur at any hour of the day or night, regardless of curfews or building security. "I cannot imagine my life without beer," he liked to say, usually while pouring another glass, affectionately monitoring the rise of the head to the rim and, often enough, over the top. Beer and peanuts on our balcony in warm weather, our activities protected by foliage, or in our living room during the cooler months, equally secure from prying eyes and ears, unless the rooms were indeed bugged, as some claimed: Zhou/Julius claimed to value dwelling in these foreign shadows more than any others – except those of his hoodlum friends.

He likewise sought the shade of an extended Tibet reverie that he liked to share with me, especially once the concrete railing, or the coffee table, boasted enough empty bottles. In this waking dream, a fantasy nurtured with middling passion before June 4th and then with a kind of desperate creativity in the months following the massacre, Zhou would vanish into the high Himalayas and onto the massive Tibetan plateau, and there would find not so much freedom from the army or the government, nor even a regenerative life among Buddhist nomads, as oblivion. An oblivion of thin, gasping air and blazing, pitiless light;

an oblivion of snow-capped peaks and funnel valleys, stone and scree and winds so sharp they left cheeks permanently rasped. No more crappy politics and blunt violence. No more bleary gazes and oozing pores.

No more Zhou Shuren, aka Julius.

Who could not imagine his life without beer.

He had another mantra. Years before, while still a student, Zhou had answered a casting call for Bernardo Bertolucci's *The Last Emperor.* The film, one of the earliest western productions given permission to shoot inside the Peoples' Republic of China, needed a young male with slangy English for a small speaking part. The role was of a Red Guard charged with marching a disgraced teacher through the streets of the capital during a Cultural Revolution humiliation parade. In the scene, the last Qing emperor, Pu Yi, having experienced a humane 're-education' at the hands of that teacher a decade earlier, steps forth from the crowd to testify to the man's character. The Red Guard intercepts the former deity, listens to his pleas for compassion and historical per-spective, and then advises: "Join the revolution, Comrade, or else fuck off."

Zhou got the part.

He rehearsed the line for weeks. Over and over, with friends and family and strangers in the streets. The day of the shoot was bliss. Lights, cameras and action, along with free food on the set. Plus the West – western efficiency and magnetism, western art and even celeb-rity, in the form of Bertolucci himself – right there before him, a tanta-lizing sighting, brief and strange and, I gathered, eternally unsettling. Because, nearly five years after that single-day experience as a cast member of *The Last Emperor,* Zhou was still rehearsing the line. Only now the dialogue had evolved into a catch-all to summarize both the absurdity of China and, in his darker, more beery moods, his own wast-rel existence. Asked about almost anything – the filth in the faculty dor-mitory hallways or the decision of his department not to fix their one film projector; the suspension of classes during the student protests in April or the ominous announcement of martial law in late May – and Zhou Shuren would shake hair from his eyes and grin his slow, crooked-toothed grin. "Join the revolution, Comrade," he would answer, "or else . . . "

These were our friends on the campus in East Beijing where my wife and I were teaching in the spring of 1989. Friends who went to march downtown with their fellow professors and students, knowing their photos were being taken and their names recorded by spies. Friends who, if not already missing from their rooms or our apartment the night of June 3rd and into the morning of the 4th, and if not already exhausted from attempting to block soldiers passing the campus gate en route to Tiananmen Square, hopped onto their bicycles and raced the six miles into the city, to see if the terrible rumours could possibly be true.

II

A handful of people first staged turmoil, which later developed into a counter-revolutionary rebellion. Their aim was to overthrow the Communist Party, topple the socialist system, and establish a bourgeois republic.

—DENG XIAOPING, JUNE 9, 1989

"What are you rebelling against?" I called to Zhou Shuren one day in April. He was on a bike, making for the south gate and the road into Beijing, where students were gathering on Tiananmen Square to commiserate the death of a Party elder. Zhou slowed at the chance to deliver another movie line in English. "Whaddya got?" he replied, channelling Marlon Brando. I scarcely saw him during the next six weeks, the beer in our fridge sitting untouched. By early May, with crowds on the square swelling less with college kids than factory workers and government employees, along with people from outside the capital come to see if history was indeed being made, Zhang Naiying proposed a theory to explain the escalation of a student protest into a general strike. "Ordinary Chinese like to enjoy the beautiful weather," she said to us. "They can eat ice cream and drink juice." I was incredulous. "That's the only reason they're marching around Tiananmen Square all day?" I asked. "Actually, it's quite a lot,"

Naiying – aka Francis – answered, speaking with the authority of a native. "Beijingers have little opportunity to participate in civic events."

A week later, on the day Tiananmen Square hosted a million jovial insurrectionists, many in fact eating ice cream and most seeming to bask as much in the glorious sunlight as in the astonishing recklessness of their actions, I asked Shu Sheyu if China was changing. "I am not sure about China," he said. "But I think I am." He marched along Changan Avenue the following afternoon with other faculty members, his limp causing him to drift from the front row back into the pack, like a slower animal in a herd.

Shortly after Martial Law was announced, with rumours swirling of tank brigades pressing on Beijing under instructions to clear Tiananmen Square by any means, a quaking, moist-eyed Ding Luojin visited our apartment. "Protestors are chanting 'The Peoples' Army don't Attack the People," she said, chewing on her pigtail. "Do people believe that?" my wife asked. "I don't think so," she replied very softly. We pleaded with her to stay on campus, offering our kitchen for cooking and our couch for reading novels all day and night, as enticements. She said she would have to talk to her roommates; whatever they resolved to do, even if it included dying on the square, would be okay with her.

Forty-eight hours after the massacre, Zhou Shuren knocked on our door at midnight. He was dressed in a Mao suit and had cropped his hair. Refusing a beer, he paced the living room. "The police are looking for me," he said. "I must leave Beijing." Explaining that he had bunked for the two weeks of Martial Law at the art institute where the 'Goddess of Democracy' statue was created, he confessed that he had also stayed on Tiananmen until near sunrise on June 4th, defying tanks and APCs, and then had helped carry the wounded and the dead to hospitals and morgues. He sobbed, staring down at his hands. "Where will you go?" I eventually asked. "Tibet," he replied, instinctively brushing hair from his eyes. "Canada. Iceland. It doesn't matter." We expressed feeble condolences. "China is shit," Zhou Shuren said, his gaze briefly blazing. "Only crazy people live here, or stupid people like me."

III

A country of weaklings, even if they have guns, can only massacre un-armed people; if the enemy is also armed, the issue is uncertain. Only then is true strength and weakness revealed.

—LU XUN

In January, 1990, back at the same Beijing college, living in the same building and teaching mostly the same classes, with our colleagues, having endured an autumn of demotions, criticisms and re-educations, likewise returned to their jobs in an atmosphere of such fear and gloom that the sun hid away for a month in sympathy; in this setting, I decided to read as much Lu Xun as I could find. Lu (1881-1936) is essential to an understanding of China. A great artist, he is also that rarest of icons: one who survived his enshrinement in the Communist pantheon of 'revolutionary' culture-makers with his integrity, and even his words, intact. Mao Zedong, whose admiration of real art did not extend much beyond its usefulness to his own ambitions, had only praise for Lu Xun. In 1940, while still a rebel leader, Mao enshrined the recently deceased author with an essay extolling Lu's prescient radicalism. That piece of writing – titled, simply, 'An Essay on Lu Xun' – was, like most of the Chairman's jottings, later studied and memorized, recited in classrooms or from within fitful sleeps, by generations. Lu's novella, 'The Real Story of Ah Q,' was similarly rendered immortal by its inclusion on school reading lists, starting after liberation.

'Ah Q,' for instance, originally published in 1919, is a savage tale of a foolish man so befuddled by hazy allegiances to unworthy masters that he winds up cheering on his own execution, believing it a splendid moment. But according to the Party line, typified by a capsule summary contained in the sanctioned English translation of Lu that I bought – a handsome four-volume hardcover edition called the *Collected Works,* on sale in western hotels and shops around Beijing for the equivalent price of a single American paperback – the story "bitterly criticizes the bourgeoisie, which led the 1911 revolution but failed to arouse the peasants."

Lu did become a communist in the 1930s. Still, the grizzly bear embrace of Chairman Mao would have both amused and alarmed him. An artist steeped in irony and the surrealism practised by 19th-century Russian author Nicoli Gogol, whose novel *Dead Souls* he revered, Lu would have issued a similarly wan smile at how earnestly and crassly his fiction came to be read. A translator himself, of Gogol and many others, he would have shaken his head at the participation of translators, including the husband-wife team of Yang Xiangyi and Gladys Yang that rendered the *Collected Works* into serviceable English, in the distortions obliged by socialist aesthetics. (Yang and Yang opted to title his epochal story collection *Call to Arms*, instead of the more accurate, if less stirring, *Cheering from the Sidelines*.) Finally, a modest, unflashy person whose personal life – an arranged marriage likely never consummated, a young lover with whom he had a child – he kept notably separate from his voluminous published writings, Lu would surely have cringed at the statues of him erected in parks and on campuses throughout China, as well as the museums in Shanghai and Beijing crammed with displays of his manuscripts and cigarette cases, robes and toiletries. As for the museum shops, where visitors could stock up on Lu Xun books and pens, buttons and pendants – those merchandising offshoots of sanctioned celebrity might well have left him at a loss for words or expressions alike.

Had Lu lived to witness liberation in 1949, by then an elder of sixty-eight, he would surely have simultaneously welcomed the overthrow of the horrendous Kuomintang government of Chiang Kai-Shek while criticizing the incoming regime of Mao Zedong for its brutality, especially the extermination campaign of 1949-50, in which as many as two million landlords were executed in order to free up their land for collectivization. A critic of false language, it is unlikely Lu would have taken much time before commenting on how low "the peasants" remained in this bold "dictatorship of the proletariat." An intuitive democrat, he would soon have wondered aloud about the steady deification of Mao Zedong himself, a process very similar to the exaltation of emperors. He would, in short, have noted the same national characteristics on display in the revolution, threatening to render it no more than a variation on a venerable Chinese theme: absolute power, once obtained and solidified, absolutely enforced.

Starting in 1949, Lu Xun would have said all this in public and written it down with his usual elegance and candour, sending his essays to the dwindling number of publications that had yet to read the censored writing on the wall about freedom of expression within the PRC. Then, still bemused – if also appalled – by the familiar patterns he was observing, he might have predicted in print his own imminent arrest and denouncement by, or on behalf of, the same Chairman Mao who had previously dubbed him immortal. I doubt Lu would have fled the country. I suspect he would have died in disgrace, possibly in prison.

I was concentrating on the two volumes of Lu Xun's essays. Though revered for his fiction, his genius may have been best served by his short essays, called *zawen*, produced for newspapers and magazines. A cross of personal column with epigrammatic philosophical essay, *zawen* suited a writer anxious to be accessible to a wide audience, not to mention one often obliged to flee a city where a warlord he had incensed had proclaimed him a dead man, and sent out assassins to provide the evidence. "Some Notes Jotted Down by Lamplight," for example, dated from 1925, the year Lu had to depart Beijing for a string of southern cities where fewer powerful people wished him harm. He begins the essay with an anecdote. During a recent period of hyperinflation in China, he reports, he traded his own currency for silver on the black market, accepting an exchange rate of just forty percent of face value. Later, when offered fifty percent by a rival trader, he found himself expressing gratitude at this 'improvement' – of, in effect, only half a loss. "How easy it is for us to become slaves," he concludes, "and to revel in our slavery!"

Three thousand years of Chinese history are condensed into two epochs. The first, eras of social anarchy, are dubbed "the periods when we longed in vain to be slaves." The second, those eras where the country was unified by a strong leader – aka a dictator wearing one uniform or another – Lu calls "the periods when we succeeded in becoming slaves for a time." What epoch is China in now? he asks of the 1920s. He recognizes that many citizens, unnerved by the disorder that has reigned since the collapse of the Qing Dynasty fourteen years before, are nostalgic for the good old days of being docile slaves to an emperor. Lu offers these people hope. "Those who hanker after the past need not feel pessimistic," he writes. "To all appearances there is still peace; for though there are often wars, droughts and floods, have you ever heard anyone raise his voice in protest?"

He shifts metaphor abruptly. "Our vaunted Chinese civilization is only a feast of human flesh prepared for the rich and mighty. And China is only the kitchen where those feasts are prepared." Cannibalism was Lu Xun's most outrageous rhetorical conceit. Like Jonathan Swift, another writer he admired, he used it sparingly but without flinching. In his story 'Medicine,' a poor family hand over their life savings to feed their dying child the 'folk remedy' of a crust of bread soaked in the blood of another human being. The remedy represents the sham of a China rendered stupid by superstition and dumb custom. The family are that nation's latest sacrifices.

But in 'Some Notions Jotted Down by Lamplight' Lu disavows even the slim metaphorical protection of fiction. The Chinese, he says, are "intoxicated" by their own civilization. They crave the numbness brought on by this intoxication, with its implicit sanction of barbarism. "They cannot feel each other's pain," he comments of Chinese society, "and because each can hope to enslave and eat other men, he forgets he may be enslaved and eaten himself." He ends with a warning: "Feasts of human flesh are still being spread even now and many people will want them to continue."

The essay, barely 1500 words in length, also finds space to issue a plea to foreigners who interact with China. Westerners, Lu complains, are forever lauding the Chinese for their excellent culture and enigmatic but splendid traditions. He decries this tendency of foreigners *not* to criticize their hosts. By remaining aloof, the rest of the world is, by default, encouraging the nation to stay in bondage. He gives an example. The British philosopher Bertrand Russell had recently visited the Middle Kingdom. According to Lu Xun, Russell "praised the Chinese when some sedan-chair bearers smiled at him." Of this glancing incident, he makes two requests: that the "chair bearers stop smiling at their fares" and that westerners cease admiring uncritically all things Chinese, including the submissiveness of impoverished rickshaw drivers. That kind of admiration, he implies, masks either condescension – the secret view that China remains a child among the men of nations – or else marks a hangover from the 19th-century European fashion of oriental exoticism, which objectified the country as silky, mysterious and feral, an adventure-travel destination that promised plenty of moral, social and even sexual *frissons*.

I sat up at Lu's twin directives. "Some Notions," born of rage at how authority was exercised and dissent suppressed in 1920s China, could have as easily been birthed from June 4th. Fearing they would be eaten, Deng Xiaoping and his generals – the rich and mighty, in effect – had feasted instead on their own children. Their paranoia had also trickled down into society, including the student protestors. When three young teachers tossed ink-filled eggs at the portrait of Chairman Mao on Tiananmen Square during a demonstration, student leaders, worried the pranksters were undercover agents sent to disgrace the movement, had them detained. They even volunteered the egg throwers to the police. The teachers, accidentally betrayed by their own, were given lengthy jail terms, including a life sentence for the instigator, a twenty-seven-year-old named Yu Zhijian.

Similarly, when a Beijinger provided an eyewitness account of the massacre to an international television crew, authorities flashed a clip of the interview on the national evening news, urging citizens to smoke out this enemy. The next day the television showed the man, hand-cuffed and the worse for his arrest, muttering an apology to his nation for spreading lies and counter-revolutionary propaganda. Two frumpy women smiled for the camera, proud of having made a meal of their neighbour.

Lu Xun's essay may have been addressing Bertrand Russell and his fellow early century visitors, but his argument with foreigners applied equally to us. Our friends in Beijing weren't smiling for their rickshaw fares. My wife and I, in turn, were attempting to see these people as individuals: Shu Sheyu the joker and Ding Luojian the reader of foreign novels, Zhou Shuren, who could not imagine his life without beer. It wasn't hard to do. There was nothing inscrutable about our friends at the college. Quite the opposite: this generation of urbanites – the only Chinese we really knew – had gone about expressing their identities and ambitions in ways recognizable to a westerner. Television series like *River Elegy* and films such as Chen Kaige's *Yellow Earth*, the music of Cui Jian and poetry of Bei Dao, the novels of Wang Meng and Wang Shuo – all adopted aesthetics and convictions influenced by non-Chinese models. Cui Jian blended folk melodies with rock and reggae, ska and jazz. Wang Shuo wrote novels about urban dropouts, including the *liu-mengs* who had gleefully opted to fuck off, rather than join anyone's revolution, which had more in common with Jack Kerouac or, for that matter, Franz Kafka, than any of the Chinese classics. Cheng Kaige's early movies, like those of Zhang Yimou, his fellow former Red Guard and member of the filmmakers group known as the Fifth Generation, presented on screen a China muddled by unexamined traditions. *River Elegy*, a series aired on national television in 1987, used the actual Yellow River, with its meandering trajectory and unpredictable siltings, as a metaphor for the course of Han civilization over the past several thousand years. The country as muddy, in effect – muddy as its great river.

No disrespect was being shown by these artists, and certainly no one was calling for the old culture to be obliterated, as Mao Zedong himself had done for his own lunatic reasons in 1966. Among our friends a spirit of inquiry ruled, of wishing to examine through clear, widened eyes the very sober specifics of being Chinese at the end of the 20th century. In the thrall of a cultural awakening, a generation dared themselves to think and say things that made their children-of-Mao parents wince in fear and their grandparents, retaining memories of China before 1949, nod in quaking recognition. It was all giddy and reckless and without plan or precedent; a protest by Beijing students in April that included complaints about cafeteria food wound up a month later shouldering the weight of a burgeoning movement of consciousness that seemed to be calling on China to liberate itself, almost, from the prison of its own national identity.

Small wonder that mistakes were made, most notably the wheeling of the too confrontational, too alien Goddess of Democracy statue onto the square. Small wonder, too, the crackdown, when it finally came, displayed such savagery. Through the design of no one, and despite the desires of all but a few genuine anarchists, the dynamics invoked in Lu Xun's notes written in lamplight were played out in the bright, camera-friendly light of day, with the mandate of heaven – i.e. the right of the Communist Party to continue its absolutist rule – suddenly at risk.

IV

Suppose there was an iron room with no windows or doors, a room it would be virtually impossible to break out of. And suppose you had some people inside that room who were sound asleep. Before long they would all suffocate. In other words, they would slip peacefully from a deep slumber into oblivion, spared the anguish of being conscious of their impending doom. Now let's say that you came along and stirred up a big racket that awakened some of the lighter sleepers. In that case, they would go to a certain death fully conscious of what was going to happen to them. Would you say that you had done those people a favour?

—Lu Xun

In April 1990 my wife and I attended a performance at the Beijing Concert Hall. On the bill was the violin concerto 'Butterfly Lovers.' Zhang Naiying, who hummed the principal melody incessantly, insisted we hear the piece performed live. The experience, she maintained, would help us understand the nature of Chinese melancholy. Composed in 1949 by two Shanghai music students as a concerto for violin and string orchestra, 'Butterfly Lovers' had defied the slow shutting down of China to the West during the 1950s by becoming popular with everyone from the urban intelligentsia to the newly-minted rural proletariat. It helped that the music borrowed from a folk tune and retold a legend, a local version of Romeo and Juliet that featured star-crossed young lovers separated by their families – both had been promised at birth in arranged marriages – who are reunited, with all due tragedy, in the end. It helped equally that the piece, narrated mostly by a dolorous violin, was sweet and sorrowful and shameless in its minor-key tugs on emotions. Nor did it hurt that the concerto, decidedly western-decadent, had been banned during the Cultural Revolution and only cautiously re-introduced into the repertoire during the 1980s. Since June 4th, apparently, it had been once more unofficially proscribed, as if the musical expression of such broad private sentiments and deep personal feelings somehow challenged the state's view of reality – or possibly of the individual.

Twelve hundred people packed the hall, including dozens who had gained entrance without tickets and were squatting in the aisles, deaf to the harangues of ushers. Chinese audiences, accustomed to noisy all-day Peking opera performances, popped cans of soda and shelled peanuts, chatted and laughed and slipped out for cigarettes during symphonies by Beethoven and Brahms. But the hushed opening of 'Butterfly Lovers,' a flute sounding over plucked harp, induced silence and stillness. Aisle squatters ceased fidgeting. Entire rows leaned into the music. The violinist, wearing a bang of black hair and a movie star swagger, sobered upon bowing his first notes, rocking on his heels. He also whipped the bow back during pauses, as if it was in danger of catching fire. With the score straying only slightly from the lovelorn melody, the twenty minute concerto lurched from soft to loud, solo violin to full strings, the emotional shifts ranging from A to B to A again, rendering the piece more akin to a dirge or lament, circular and consoling, than to any progression of musical ideas. Expecting 'Butterfly Lovers' to end with a bang, I was stunned by its decision to finish instead on a single held note. The violin did not fade so much as recede, and I – and everyone else in the hall, I suspected – kept on hearing the melody long after the air emptied. Could silence be a ringing in the ear? It was a sound I had not heard before.

Early that summer I also travelled to Tibet. Zhou Shuren's reveries of vanishing into the desolation of the central Asian plateau had increased in intensity during the spring, along with his intake of beer. He had likewise reported on the adventures of an artist friend who, sought by police for his Tiananmen activities, had survived a forty-day overland trek into northern Tibet, and now was living in an unidentified village in an unidentified valley in a range of mountains distinguished on topographical maps by only a number. The friend, supplied a video camera the previous June by a fleeing German tourist, was making films and writing poetry up there; he was living like a reasonably free man in a reasonably free nation in a place notable, of course, for being free of both governments and human beings. Zhou should be making films in an unidentified Tibetan valley and writing poetry in an unnamed Tibetan village. Beijing was killing him. China would be his demise.

I flew to Lhasa in part to honour Zhou's reverie and in part to meet a Tibetan author named Tashi Dawa. He had published a strange tale called 'A Soul in Bondage,' available in a 1988 collection of contemporary 'Chinese' fiction translated into English. 'A Soul in Bondage', too, was like nothing I had ever read, by a Tibetan or Chinese or any other kind of writer. More strange still, the story struck me as a fictional analogue to Zhou Shuren's waking dreams and disaffections. Shu Sheyu, familiar with someone who worked for Tashi Dawa's publisher, wrote a letter on my behalf. I booked a flight into Chengdu, in Sichuan province, and there paid a fee to join a fictitious 'tour' into Tibet – the only sanctioned passage into the recalcitrant, and heavily monitored, colony.

V

It is certainly hard to live in this world. To "lack worldly wisdom" is not good, but neither is it good to have "too much worldly wisdom." Apparently worldly wisdom is like revolution. "A revolution is needed but it should not be too radical." You need some worldly wisdom, but not too much.

Once a thing is described, it has its limitations and its quintessence is lost for good. So to talk of the "quintessence of worldly wisdom" is a contradiction in terms. The truth of the quintessence is in deeds not words, yet just by saying "deeds not words" I have let slip the Truth again, and am further from the quintessence.

—Lu Xun

Having filed June 4th as a treasonous uprising, the Chinese government devoted the 1990s to ensuring that history remain obscured in a haze of coerced forgetfulness. The state made its citizenry a deal: vague material prosperity in exchange for a refutation of the vivid past. With the media supporting the revision, and the authorities tolerating no queries, never mind dissent, and with China experiencing sustained growth beyond even its own wildest projections, taking the deal seemed prudent. Tiananmen Square never happened. Six students only, along with a handful of thugs, died while resisting army and police efforts to restore order in the capital. Six! A lie, a grovel, accepted by outright slaves or by those hankering to be slaves once more? Lu Xun's 1925 question stood.

Those student leaders that escaped arrest went into hiding. Eventually, most wound up in disappointed exile in the West. Our friends, too, scattered during the years following the massacre. Shu Sheyu used a contact to get himself invited to a university in Sweden, where he settled. Zhang Naiying quit academia and found a job representing a Chinese firm in the United States. Lacking the networks, Ding Luojin still managed to slip into Shenzhen, the special economic zone bordering Hong Kong. She lived in that city before finally immigrating to Canada. Others found their way to Toronto or New York, or else dissolved into the workforce in Beijing, earning multiple times their teaching salaries as translators for international companies. Only Zhou Shuren truly vanished. Instead of Tibet, however, he disappeared into Europe, thanks to a French student who, returning to Paris after June 4th, sponsored his emigration there. I did not find out where he lived for nearly a decade.

Contact with these people ceased until email, MSN, and various passages across the Pacific Ocean rekindled the friendships. But in 1992 I published a non-fiction book about a group of Beijing intellectuals struggling in the aftermath of the democracy movement. Though I changed names (and continue to use the pseudonyms in this essay) and altered details, I portrayed Shu, Zhang, Ding, and Zhou, with frank, unabashed ardour. In an early draft of the book I also ended several chapters with images of the cooking and eating of human flesh, to underscore my – or was it Lu Xun's? – fierce commitment to the truth. An editor wisely excised the material.

Four years later I wrote a novel, set partly in Montreal and partly in China, whose title, and climactic scene, borrowed from the experience of attending that performance of 'Butterfly Lovers' in Beijing. Five years on again, at the outset of the 21st century, I published still another novel rooted in what happened the winter and spring of 1990. It tells the tale of a Canadian who travels to a country modelled on Tibet to meet the author of a beguiling short story. The Canadian lands in trouble with the authorities, as I actually did in Lhasa that June, and may have gotten the writer in even deeper and most lasting difficulty, as I did not. But imagining such an outcome wasn't difficult.

Join the revolution, comrade? I tried. I tried to prove my fidelity. Returning to Beijing was one offering of proof. Likewise the publishing of those books. Granted, it seemed ineffectual at the time, and still seems so now, with our lives redirected many times over and history still largely a muddle.

2000-2005

THE ICE CRACKING AT DAWN:

A Memoir Of 9/11

My grandfather returned from the Second World War without his nose. He lost it in Belgium, and once lost, apparently, a nose can't be recovered. He served as an officer in the Canadian army. On an inspection tour the bridge he happened to be crossing was blown up. A plank caught him in the face, making a mess.

As a child I was encouraged to touch the nose that surgeons had built for my grandfather using skin from his buttocks. It was soft and wobbly and the slit-sized air holes were purely decorative. I found the nose repellent but also interesting, like a cat stiffening by a curb. "No cartilage in there," he would explain. "Sock me one, and I won't even feel it." He also had a joke, repeated over and over: "What an ass-kisser this kid is. He'll make a great officer some day."

My grandfather's nose got left on the ground in Europe, a continent saturated in blood and guts and body parts. My father was only a boy in 1939, and only an adolescent in 1945, but he hasn't, I suspect, ever gotten over the fact that he never walked that terrain, a prospector searching a stream for rocks that glimmer. Had he gone to Europe, he would have understood more about a world where the bridge you were on might be blown up, and your features rearranged. He also might have understood, and perhaps liked, his own father more.

Instead, he grew up to be a man who met a bear in the bush. While still in his early twenties, anxious to put as many miles as he could between himself and his parent, my father ran a mining camp in Northern Ontario. One evening he was returning to the camp through the woods, using moonlight filtered through the treetops as a guide. Tucked under his arm was a .303, the barrel lowered. When something snuck up beside him and brushed the rifle, he nearly dropped it. He flinched at the stench and squinted at the outline. A black bear reared before him. He staggered, and as he did he raised the barrel and squeezed the trigger. Because the bear was on its hind legs, it took the bullet in the face. Much of the animal's skull wound up in my father's hair and over his jacket. The next morning he returned to make sure the bear was dead. The corpse had settled into the earth, bleaching the soil crimson.

I was born in 1960 in a suburb of Toronto. I knew the dead bear as a bush story and the missing nose as a war story, and both were fragments, too vague and displaced to lodge as family lore. Though I could never have articulated it, these story fragments came from worlds far away, where the ground beneath your feet was soaked in blood. I knew as well that where I lived was different. Where I lived, there was no ground beneath. Instead, there was television, and I grew up floating inside its dream, my feet in the air and features glowing.

A childhood inside TV has done me no harm. Likewise for one occurring in the suburbs, the object of so much derision among those who count themselves happy refugees from it. I don't know who else feels how I do about growing up in the late 1960s and 70s, and I don't presume to be telling a story other than my own. That would be the story of my grandfather's nose, and the son who was never given the chance to find it. Also, of my father's encounter with a bear, and the things he may have wanted to tell his own boy about – the stink of a four-hundred-pound carcass, the taste of grilled bear – but could never find the right context, the right words.

And of that boy, golden with pixel glow, the soles of his feet as soft as a baby's cheeks. A boy staring at a screen and believing it not a mirror, or a portal, but rather simply a planet – his planet, his home.

As a shortcut, I could reconstruct a TV Guide from the era, run down the programs, the days and times, the repeats and specials, and make myself understood to some. *Rocketship 7*, every afternoon from 3:30 to 5pm, hosted by Commander Tom, with *Gilligan's Island*, *Batman*, and *Superman* in rotation. Or the game shows, in their morning-to-afternoon order: *The Price is Right* and *$10,000 Pyramid*, *Joker's Wild* and *Hollywood Squares*.

Best to explain, though, using an American rabbit and a Chinese philosopher. Bugs Buggy roamed wild in my imagination. He was a smart, funny rabbit, and he could outwit any Daffy Duck or Elmer Fudd. *The Bugs Bunny-Road Runner Hour*, Saturdays at five, was watched without fail, even after Saturday afternoon mass became an acceptable substitute for Sunday mornings. By then, I was maybe ten and knew all the cartoons line-for-line. I knew Bugs's excellent put downs and I knew his mischievous good heart.

He spoke to me once. It happened in church. I was waiting in the pews with some other Grade Fives for altar boy lessons. In front of us was the sacristy, the side-altar where the tabernacle, housing the bread and wine used during mass, is kept. Our church had a neat design feature – a hole carved into the low stucco ceiling above the sacristy. Down from the hole poured a stream of light that bathed the tabernacle in a saintly shaft.

A friend dared me to look up the hole. I figured I would see Jesus in there, his chest cracked open to reveal a meaty red heart, which we all kept breaking with our sins. I worried I might encounter his Dad, bearded and bug-eyed and wielding a stick. My knees buckled thinking about him.

But it proved lovely inside the sacristy light: soft and smothering and closer to sleep than wakefulness. Lovely, like the way watching television in the den on a Saturday morning could be, the snow falling outside and the rest of the house still slumbering. At once I knew I wouldn't meet anything scary. I knew it would be another nice experience in my nice life. The light did sting my eyes a bit, like a candle flame studied up close for too long, but I squinted, rubbed them, and squinted more. I saw smoke. I saw a blazing centre to the beam, a glare more powerful than any car hood reflecting sunshine at midday. That I could not look at, of course, being just a kid. That was God.

Then I saw Bugs. Inside the shaft, upside-down, in his standard pose – legs crossed, an elbow propping up his one-ear-floppy head. "Eh, what's up, Doc?" he asked, munching a carrot.

The ancient Chinese philosopher Lao Zhi was not a name I recognized until I was well into my twenties. But earlier, at sixteen or seventeen, I read a version of his famous parable. Lao Zhi falls asleep by a stream and dreams he is a butterfly. Upon waking, he wonders: Am I a man who has just dreamed he is a butterfly, or am I a butterfly dreaming he is a man?

While I didn't understand the parable – this was different from the ones taught to us at mass, like the story of the good Samaritan – I felt certain it applied to me. It was about staring out my basement bedroom window, watching nothing much happen on the street. It was about shooting baskets in the driveway at dusk and cutting the lawn in the rain. The parable was also about walking to school every day past other houses with basement windows and basketball nets, and other teenage boys pushing lawnmowers over slick grass. The butterfly/man conundrum was about how my life *felt*, in effect, and I was happy to discover that some people, including Chinese philosophers, shared the feeling.

Could I explain it? Not exactly. Of being alone, but not lonely. Of being solitary, but not isolated. Of never being sure if I was awake and dreaming or asleep and dreaming of being awake, and thinking that was okay.

So I watched television after school and on weekends, sometimes with my brother and sister, often by myself. So my grandfather died at age sixty-four, a man I barely knew, aside from the rubbery texture of his nose, because he was the father that his son could never forgive. (Also, because they never walked the battlefields of Europe together?) So my father, once a bear killer, left for work in a suit at seven in the morning and returned home at seven in the evening, and might watch some TV later on, after the kids were in bed. I would come out of my room, claiming I couldn't sleep, just to sit beside him on the couch and sip his coffee, though it tasted awful, and pretend to smoke his pipe, despite how the bitter air pricked at my brain.

Because he never took me hunting, and put me on a path with a black bear?

In college I read the Russians. Of the major poets, Osip Mandelstam's lean, alert poems had the most effect. "I hear, I hear the ice cracking at dawn," Mandelstam wrote in one lyric. Then there was the Stalin epigraph, which probably cost the poet his life. "We live, not feeling the land beneath us," Mandelstam declared. "Our speech inaudible ten steps away. "

A light went on in my mind. There it was: the metaphor I needed to understand how I had been shaped by a childhood with television. To live, not feeling the land beneath. To awake, never hearing the ice cracking outside. To not possess, in short, a relationship with my society, with my age. To not be alive, with everyone else, in a field of bloody soil and missing body parts.

Was there any other way to understand the world, and yourself? To understand your father, and so – again – yourself?

I have children now, two daughters. I am forty-one, and have still never gone into the bush with my father. I called my parents on September 11th, having just watched tower two of the World Trade Center collapse on – what else? – TV. They had done the same from their farm, where they settled into retirement after leaving the suburb. We shared our horror and dismay, and then said it was good to hear each others' voices, to know that everyone was safe. My kids were asleep – in the vertical Asian city where I currently live, it was evening when the terrorists attacked – otherwise I would have asked them to speak with their grandfather. He could have explained what had happened better than their parent. He could have talked about hearing the ice crack at dawn and no longer feeling the land beneath your feet.

To my father, I should have said this: I don't miss the house I grew up in and I don't miss the basement where I watched TV. But I miss him, and have been lonely for him, on some strange, sub-terrain level, a current that I am only now registering in the soles of my feet, only now beginning to feel rise up into my body, an ache that might just be the ache of loss, all my life.

To my daughters, I should have said this: It was nice, how I was raised, awake inside my own dream. It was nice – everyone should be so lucky – and I'm even sorry it had to end.

2002

WHY YOU SHOULD TRAVEL:

A Family in 9/11 Asia

Alongside our thirty thousand neighbours, I live with my family in a high-rise complex on the south side of Hong Kong Island. Thirty-four towers, all around forty storeys in height, overlook the South China Sea. Along the waterfront is a U-shaped boardwalk offering vistas of outer islands and sparkling ocean. Residents stroll the boardwalk at most hours of the day and late into the evening. The air is considered just about the cleanest in Hong Kong. The sights – container vessels out in the shipping lanes, local trawlers rounding the bend from Aberdeen harbour – are routine but pleasing. An American aircraft carrier drifted silently by once, as surreal as the floating island in *Gulliver's Travels*. Seagulls bob atop Styrofoam containers, poised as ballerinas.

Walkers and joggers, kids on bikes and old men with bamboo fishing poles and fuming cigarettes carry on beneath the outer ring of buildings. I jog there most afternoons. My route obliges me to run in the lee of several towers and thus in the path of any objects that might fall from a window perch or sill. Cast shadows don't hurt, but dropped flowerpots can split open a skull. A coin plummeting from the twentieth floor apparently lands like a hammer blow.

Then there are the bodies. Hong Kong has a notorious suicide rate, and leaping is the means of oblivion of choice. Though local newspapers tend to bury accounts of these tragedies in the news-item pages, they often include a sentence expressing sombre communal admiration if the jumper has waited until the off hours, thus sparing pedestrians below unpleasantness or injury. It takes a celebrity leap, like the suicide of pop star Leslie Cheung during the recent SARS crisis, to grab and hold a headline. Cheung plummeted from the top of a five-star hotel in Central on the first day of April. But even he was careful to choose a traffic-only side of the building and to wait for a pause in the flow. Fans who kept vigil outside the hotel for weeks after his death, arranging flowers and photos, old album jackets and VHS cassettes, into an ad hoc shrine, noted this final courtesy as well. Leslie Cheung died a respectful Hong Kong boy.

Regardless, jog beneath enough high-rises where residents routinely position plants on sills and hang washing out to dry and one is bound to eventually encounter pairs of pants or smashed pots of palms on the asphalt. I stride over plenty of socks on my runs and get dripped on by leaky air conditioners. Nothing bigger or heavier has fallen so far, but it could, anytime. Forever startling is the sight of a Filipino maid balancing on a window ledge while washing windows two hundred feet above the earth, like the blind prince feeling his way towards the cliff edge at the end of Akira Kirosawa's *Ran*. The great Japanese director was positing an existential question with this tableau; the maid is attempting to clear bird droppings from the glass before her employer returns from another stressful day at the office.

There is, in other words, a degree of risk involved in even the most mundane activities in this most secure and prosperous of Asian cities. It isn't a big risk, and Hong Kongers abide by a vertical-dwelling code of civility and safety – as well as stoicism, in the instances of the jumpers – but it is still real.

Issues of chance and risk have kept my waking thoughts company these past eighteen months. The region we presently call home has not been spared fallout from the terrorist attacks in America, or the subsequent coalition invasions of Afghanistan and Iraq. Last fall, a bomb in Bali killed two hundred people, half of them Australians. Two American teachers living in Papua, an eastern province of Indonesia, were executed in August, possibly by rogue military elements, while an Illinois missionary kidnapped by Islamic rebels in the southern Philippines died during an army raid aimed at freeing him and his wife. Even sleepy Laos has been implicated. Gunmen believed to be linked with a separatist movement there staged a roadside ambush in February, killing ten, including two Swiss cyclists.

My wife and I like to travel with our daughters during school holidays. In September we booked flights for Christmas in Bali. On October 11, 2002, bombs went off in Kuta, a popular beach strip outside the Balinese capital, Denpasar. The largest device was stored in a van in a nightclub district. Two bars favoured by expatriates were incinerated, with many of the victims blown, literally, to smithereens. The bombs, planted by terrorists belonging to an Islamic fundamentalist cell based on the neighbouring island of Java, were aimed at vacationing Westerners, in retribution for crimes both specific and general. Because of this, a number of nations, including Canada, immediately issued travel advisories against visiting Bali. The island cleared of tourists and their cash.

For weeks we followed the debate about whether or not Bali was "safe." The tone was dispiriting. The island is singular, a contemporary society where people live by, and for, their faith, but without the distorting fury that now seems so often to accompany deep religiosity. All the distinctive qualities of the culture, including its reputation for gentleness and tolerance, or even the fact that the Balinese are Hindus, worshippers of Shiva, Brahma and Ganesh and readers of the Upanishads and the Ramayana, were lost to one admittedly graphic headline: Westerners had once again been targeted and killed by extremists. This made the place dangerous, in certain eyes. This made it too high a risk.

Southeast Asians had already begun questioning the politics of travel advisories. Mahathir Mohamad, the prime minister of Malaysia, used a regional conference to lash out at the United States and Australia for their post-9/11 warnings to their citizens. Mahathir resented Malaysia's inclusion on various lists, calling concerns about tourist safety "baseless" and a kind of economic sabotage. How, Asians argued, could the American government declare Malaysia unsafe but not New York? Within weeks of the destruction of the World Trade Center, campaigns were encouraging tourists to return to the city, both to reinvigorate the economy and deny the terrorists any satisfaction. Yet the State Department then turned around and warned Americans away from Bangkok and Kuala Lumpur? New Yorkers couldn't understand how anyone could think their town was dangerous, despite the three thousand dead. Balinese felt the same about their island, despite the bombs. Western travellers, of course, were far more inclined to listen to New York than Bali, and act – or not act, more likely – accordingly. The 'First World' almost never sees itself in any other 'world,' regardless of the resemblances.

I recognized this bias. I was also familiar with the chasm between how places seem from afar versus how they look up close. Years before, a book I was writing about Northern Ireland obliged repeated visits to Belfast, where my story was situated. Almost inevitably, my departure would be preceded by a bomb going off in the city centre or a string of sectarian assassinations in one of the tribal enclaves. Canadian friends, their irises widened by television footage of the carnage, would call up with pleas that I cancel the trip until things cooled down. It was too risky. Risky and unpredictable. The facts were this: bullets in Belfast came without the names of targets carved into their shells. Bombs were less discriminating still.

That was true, up to a point. But even more truthful for me, as a visitor to the city since the late 1970s, were the 'facts' of the family whose experiences were forming my narrative spine and whose courage and resilience would, I hoped, lend the book authenticity. Those experiences were at once remarkable and ordinary. One morning a middle-class Catholic businessman and father might wake up inside his brick house in the Lower Antrim Road to hear on BBC Northern Ireland or read in the Belfast News that a middle-class Catholic businessman and father in a brick house two miles, one mile, or even just a few hundred meters away, had responded to a knock the previous evening and, upon opening his door, been gunned down by masked gunmen, in front of his wife and children. How would the father and businessman respond to this news? He might silently feel dismay and sadness at one more senseless death. If so inclined, he might say a few prayers – three Hail Marys and an Our Father, perhaps – for the dead, regardless of whether he had known the victim personally or was especially devout.

Next he would probably brew a pot of tea, bringing cups upstairs to his still-slumbering family, and then sip from a mug while standing at the kitchen counter skimming the newspaper. He would comb his hair and knot his tie, let the dog out and the cat in. Opening first the front door and then the front yard gate, he would walk to his car at the curb. The parking brake would be released and the ignition turned. First gear would be shifted into second as he accelerated down the street.

This was how people in Belfast lived through their Troubles. Not those fragments-of-the-Troubles deemed worthy of international media regard and the basis for outside diagnostics regarding the state of a society and its occupants: the rest of the days and nights and days again, lived locally. What other choice did they have? They were still alive. They were still right there.

In the end, we flew to Bali as scheduled. The island was subdued, smiles abbreviated by worry, but otherwise as gracious and welcoming as ever. Our kids played with monkeys at Uluwatu and had their hair braided on the beach at Sanur. Climbing the slopes of Gunung Agung to reach the temple-city of Pura Besakih, a guide reminded us that, even at this most revered of sites, it is not the shrines that are sacred but the spirits occupying them.

At a restaurant in Sanur a waiter named Wayan launched into an unprompted soliloquy on, of all things, Hong Kong's suicide problem. Wayan, a wiry man with precise gestures and a resolute gaze, wanted to talk. To contextualize his remarks, he first summarized his own life. Though just twenty-six, he already had two small children to feed and a sick wife who could not work. A beloved older brother had recently died. His grandfather over in Java, too, was terminally ill, and though Wayan desperately wished to see him again before his time came, he had no money for the ferry ride across the strait. Business, meanwhile, was slow: too few tourists to be shared among too many restaurants and resorts.

Regardless, he couldn't fathom why anyone would jump out his or her apartment window. Karma teaches that all you can do is behave honourably in the incarnation you have been given. No matter how humble or difficult. No matter how unjust. Wayan prayed for the bomb victims every morning, and his restaurant's daily offerings, posited near the doorway, included rice and flowers for the dead. Elegant private shrines are ubiquitous outside homes and businesses across Bali. Everyone is always praying for someone or to something.

Near Ubud, a woman named Putu said our ride in her clapped-out van was her first scrap of business since the tragedy nearly three months before. Her souvenir shop had burned down the previous summer, she explained at my prompting, and she had neither insurance nor a husband to help her rebuild. Putu had been getting by ever since as a cab driver and tour guide, not exactly her areas of expertise, especially given her struggles to use the English she had learned so long ago in high school. But she had three small children and was the family breadwinner. Days she spent seeking jobs from the scatterings of tourists. Nights she cooked, minded her kids, prayed.

Because it was New Year's Day when we met, Putu decided that our four-dollar fare was auspicious. Everything happened for a reason, she believed, folding her hands in her lap outside our hotel, and we must accept. The bombs had been a challenge to her faith. She had needed weeks to reconcile the shame she felt on behalf of all Bali, a shame undiminished by the truth that the terrorists had been both Muslim and from another part of Indonesia, interlopers come to the island with the sole intention of damaging it. Morning trips to her local temple with offerings for the victims had helped her to endure, if not to understand. She felt no anger towards the perpetrators, only a lingering sadness. It is hard to live in this world, Putu admitted.

While in Bali I read a novel whose climax sounded strange fictional echoes of the bombings in October. *Platform*, by Michel Houellebecq, was first published in France in 1999. In a key scene westerners are lounging at an Asian resort when men burst in and spray them with gunfire. Moments later a bomb goes off in a bar also favoured by expatriates. The device is hidden inside a sports bag stuffed with bolts and nails, and the force of the explosion collapses the building down onto the victims. The date of the fictional assault is given as January 2002, and the terrorists, who have already kidnapped and executed a mixed-race couple for contravening Islamic laws, are described by Houllebecq as "wearing turbans."

Among the wounded is the novel's anti-hero, Michel. He is a Parisian civil servant with a bad case of "millennial lassitude." Racist and nihilistic, alienated from all creatures living and dead, Michel is offered up as a prototypical European, reeking of "selfishness, masochism, and death." Worse still, because he is French, he broods at length about his diseased soul. "Society," Michel admits cheerfully, "could not continue to survive long with individuals like me."

Joyless copulation is his one abiding passion. When *Platform* opens Houllebecq's Christian namesake has been reduced to getting himself off on peep shows and pornography. His luck changes during a holiday in Thailand, where he meets a sexy "good predator" named

Valerie. She works in the international travel industry. Back in Paris the couple initiate a romantic tango set to the tune of S&M and public fellatio. At work, meanwhile, Valerie and her boss devise a can't-miss scheme: organized sex tours to poor countries.

Their thinking is straightforward. The First World has a narcissism parasite and plenty of cash to feed it. In the Third World, people have "nothing left to sell except their bodies." Why not offer packaged tours to those grotesque, pot-bellied Germans already groping Thai girls in bars in Bangkok and Pattaya? Why not extend the fantasy to include fulfilling the needs of moneyed gays and lesbians as well? The appetites of morally bankrupt hedonists are a market begging to be exploited.

Isn't this how capitalism operates? the novel insists. Isn't it, moreover, what chronic affluence and spiritual vacuity have done to the West – left it decadent and brutal and numb? All that remains now is to impose our "values" on the rest of the planet. Screw them every which way. Have a ball while making a big, big mess.

Houellebecq is practised in the art of literary provocation. *Platform* doesn't only crave to enrage and offend; with any luck, the book might just earn its author a *fatwa*. One part satire and one part screed, with a hefty dose of glib nihilism tossed into the tonal mix, the novel is also in rhetorical fifth gear from page one, a speed it cannot maintain on its small tank of inspiration. By the time those turbaned extremists lay waste to the resort, Houellebecq has little bile left to expel. Michel himself is certainly calm in the end. Death, he predicts, "will do me no harm."

Reading the novel in Bali was like holding a mirror up to my own image, and seeing nothing, and then holding it outwards, and still finding a blank. Though I was vacationing in exactly the kind of hapless victim nation envisioned by *Platform*, I barely recognized the landscape the author described. Though a Western male, I was likewise unfamiliar with his hideous characters, except from reading other similarly dyspeptic books and watching equally excoriating movies. Bali, it was true, wasn't the first port of call for Asian sex tourists. In Thailand, the Philippines and Cambodia, affluent adults could, and did, pay a few dollars to have sex with impoverished women and men, and sometimes girls and boys. Some travelled from distant Europe and North

America to do their damage. Most hailed from nearby China and Japan – a point of geography that is grim but still worth noting.

Whatever their country of origin, these predators still constitute only a fraction of the international visitors to any country in any of the three worlds. In my experience, people like Michel and Valerie are at best thoughtless and callow human beings, at worst actual damaged goods themselves. They are also as pathetic and as destructive at home as they are abroad. Not that most people in most places would even be aware of this equal-opportunity uselessness. Shade appreciates shadow. For some, the scrutiny of light is to be avoided at any cost.

The same holds true, I suspect, for religious fanatics. They hardly represent Islam. Many of them may well occupy the same low character rungs within their own societies. That, or else vulnerable, insecure young adults are being cajoled and coerced into participating in catastrophic acts for causes and complaints they can scarcely sort through in their own minds. Houellebecq, lacking the patience or perhaps inclination for genuine moral complexity in his fiction, sticks close to characters – grotesques, really, drawn from Moliere, via Celine and Genet – belonging to that shadowland. No harm there, except when he declares the actions of cartoon creeps indicative of broad cultural attitudes and behaviours. A crowd of louche Germans prey on Thai girls and suddenly all Westerners in Asia are sex predators? Fanatics, both fictional and real, blow up a bar in the name of Allah and now all Muslims are zealots?

Thus deepens the pan-paranoia and simmering hysteria engendered by September 11, 2001. I'm extreme, you're extreme: behold the dangerous distortion we are crafting in the various mirrors being held up to our age.

Since 9/11, commentators in Europe and beyond have been rolling their eyes at American fears over the present instability. Welcome, the mockery infers, to where the rest of us have been living all our lives. The observation is sour but truthful. Chronic affluence, especially in post-WW II United States and Canada, bred an aloofness and detachment from the larger storms out there in what North Americans sometimes dub, with varying degrees of irony, the 'R.O.P.' – the Rest of the Planet. Extremist breaching of the proverbial city on the hill has induced a nervous disorder among certain of its occupants, who still seem convinced they were not born to the same oxygen-rich atmosphere as natives of Africa or India or nearby South America. Remarkably, that false-feeling of exceptionalism can even extend to North Americans dwelling temporarily out in the R.O.P. There are few sights more dismaying than that of worldly diplomats, international businessmen and the rest of the globalized crowd fleeing a city where they have lived – generally in a level of comfort and, unsurprisingly, isolation, nearly the replica of 'back home' – at the first premonition of local troubles.

Fleeing the mayhem, be it actual or hyperventilated, is no longer that easy. Flee from where to, exactly, where else? It would be ridiculous to assert the democratization of risk in our new century. Fair, though, to remark on the widening of both actual social instability across continental and developmental divides, and the perception of it. Bombs go off in all sorts of places these days, some rich and stable, others poor and beleaguered, and will, one senses, continue to do so for some time. The days of regional exception may be over.

This being the case, why not welcome the opportunity to make a few assertions borne of our new shared landscape. That these assertions will be, for most of us, modest and private needn't diminish their value. Take my afternoon runs beneath those Hong Kong apartment towers. I am happy for the chance to go about my business confident, or maybe simply hopeful, that no one will drop an ashtray on my head. But then, why would I even be worrying about this? Mindless violence, like political extremism, is a minority response. None of my friends and neighbours, or even the people I meet in the course of most days, seem the kind to blow up bars or pay for sex tours. Of course, everyone is a little shaded, inclined to weakness and drawn to certain patches of dark, but most of us can brave the scrutiny of the light with our heads held high. We're regular people, you and me. Why should any of us be afraid?

2003

PRAY TO THE LORD OF THE LOTUS:

Floating In Old Siam

Days and nights are strange in Hong Kong. Schools have been closed for five weeks to be scrubbed free of SARS. Parents, fearful the virus will go airborne, shelter their children indoors. Playgrounds are forlorn and play dates too great a risk. With shops and restaurants likewise emptied, gloomy April weather mirrors the doom in local eyes – all that is readable on faces swathed in surgical masks.

In our apartment, waiting for the crisis to abate wears on moods in daylight and on dreams after dark. Nine-year-old Claire, a fitful sleeper, is awakened by visions of stuffed animals sprung to life. She crawls into her parents' bed and, soon after, her father retreats to the couch. There I lay, sleepless or in some in-between state, the cracked windows allowing shipping channel sounds in: the bleat of a tanker horn, the chainsaw of a fishing vessel. Water laps against the boardwalk below during quiet spells.

I dream one night of a stone carving in a jungle. The carving is the ruin of a massive hand, just three fingers surviving, the tips chewed away. Strewn over one knuckle are a scattering of flowers. Around the base are chunks of stone and tall grass. As I am just back from Cambodia, I decide the carving must belong in the temple-city of Angkor, where a friend and I lingered, easy as water lilies in a pond. In the dream the hand, belonging, presumably, to a gargantuan deity, is folded into a Buddhist *mudra*. The five Buddhas of Wisdom indicate through the crooking of their fingers which of the fundamental insights – against anger, envy, desire, ignorance or pride – they wish to teach. But then a trawler roars past the window, and the *mudra* stays unread.

In the morning I propose a trip. Forget the gloom of Hong Kong; we should go wait in Bangkok, city of eternal smiles. Certain Asian neighbours are imposing fourteen-day quarantines on Hong Kongers seeking to flee their epidemic. But friendly Thailand requests only that SARS arrivals be probed for fever at the airport, a mild gauntlet to run.

The trip takes twenty-four hours to organize. Such is our determination that neither my wife nor I check the weather. Late April, we are informed by a fellow passenger on the empty jet, marks the hottest spell of the year. Heat that softens pavement and collapses dogs onto boulevards. Heat that scorches eyelids and bores holes into exposed skulls, the better to let the hallucinations in and out.

Or the reveries, I reply to the stranger, feeling buoyant. We have cast off from plague shores and are sailing to a new land. Dark dreams lie behind us; up ahead are new ones, certain to be bright.

We reach our hotel at midday. It sits on the west bank of the Chao Praya, near the Sirin Thon bridge, four kilometres upstream from the palace roofs and temple spires of tourist Bangkok. Disregarding the hour, I insist on a walk around the neighbourhood behind the building. The vaulting sky is pale and the sun is remote and, at first squint, harmless, despite the fact that I seem to be looking at it through nylon. The air resists my passage and a breeze blows up a subway vent of vapours. Below my feet the sidewalk is spongy.

Fifteen minutes outdoors and my head begins to ache across the brow. The throb soon spreads up and over my skull, a monk's cap of pain in keeping with the botched operation underway: a drilling into bone using the blunt chisel of sunlight and the hammer of no shade. Retreating from the assault, I wince at the hotel lobby air conditioning and flop onto a bed in our room.

"My brain is boiling," I say to my wife.

"What a surprise," she replies.

Her bitterness has a history. My skin is too freckled and my ancestry too Irish for extreme sunlight. Also, I don't wear hats.

"At least it isn't SARS," I say.

"Join the girls in the pool," she says. "It might help."

The hotel pool is on a third floor terrace, exposed to the trepanning sky. Our daughters have it to themselves. Wearing swimsuits and floppy hats, bronzed skin flashing against happy grins, they play a make-believe game involving splashes and shouts. I slip into water icy as an arctic sea – or so it feels.

"Dad's on fire again," Anna says. She is twelve.

"Float, Dad," Claire says.

I do so, first on my stomach, like a corpse, and then on my back, crucified. Both positions submerge my ears, leaving my children as distant as a bad cellphone connection. The state is pleasing, a release from body weight and heavy thoughts alike, the responsibilities that accompany motion.

"What are we going to do?" Claire asks once I re-emerge.

"Swim some more."

"And then?"

"A boat ride down the river."

"And then?"

"Another ride back up."

At five o'clock we walk to the taxi stop next to the bridge. Though I am rested and have swallowed a half-dozen aspirin, I still wobble, an unsteadiness that will last for days and inflect successive nights. A dog lounges at the foot of the platform. When Anna pets it between the ears, the dog rises, tail wagging but rear legs lame. The girls go quiet as the creature drags itself to where two saffron-robed monks, one old and the other young, sit on a bench, ignoring the pitch of the dock, caused by a passing barge. The dog collapses at their sandalled feet, and we all, human and canine, exchange Thai smiles.

A long wooden boat approaches, belching diesel. Using a sequence of whistles, the conductor instructs the driver how to align the rear of the ferry with the platform. Passengers must cross a gap to board, and be mindful that the distance can abruptly widen. I step across to the deck with Claire in my grip, only to have her pull back in fright and nearly slip.

"You almost left me behind!" she says.

"The monks would have looked after you," I answer.

Before we can find seats in the open cabin the ticket lady asks our destination, to calculate the fare. For the first time I acknowledge that we don't have one. Not for this river ride, not for the trip.

Our guidebook lists the stops along the route. I name the final dock and hand her a bill.

The brown river races below the gunnels and the sun, lately turned tangerine, lays a shimmering path for the driver to follow. High noon glare causes the Grand Palace to glint, blinding admirers. Towards nightfall the buildings are more radiant, with Wat Arun and Wat Pho, most celestial of the temples, serene and resolved, like the faces of children awoken by bird call. Once it is dark a new kind of light paves the surface.

"When the moon is full it means God is watching us," Claire says, her skin cast in marble. "When it's half full he is only half watching."

"I bought travel insurance at the airport in Hong Kong," I whisper to my wife. "I'm not even sure why." She squeezes my hand.

Nearly a week floats by, pleasing and forgetful. We ride boats down and up the Chao Praya. We smile at dockside monks and lame dogs. Though pink-cheeked Germans swim in the hotel pool most mornings, the heat soon drives them indoors, leaving it for the girls to play make-believe in and their parents to be re-baptized as beings without substance. "What are we going to do next?" they stop asking. "We're not sure," we stop having to reply. The daily English newspaper confirms Hong Kong's ongoing dilemma, pressuring no timetable for return. Thick drapes and turbine air conditioning render our room a cave, ideal for deep, abandoned sleeps. Our balcony at sunrise, meanwhile, affirms the lightness of being here instead. "I can't remember what I was doing a week ago today," Mary says.

None of us escape our old selves. More unsettled than she will admit by events, my wife spars with her daughters over matters not for my ears. Missing her routine, Anna is prone to moods, especially the afternoon a dog she tries to pet snaps at her, baring teeth as jagged as Himalayan pinnacles. One night Claire calls out for help in the dark. "The monk gave me an apple," she says. "Should I eat it?" Switching on a lamp, I study her expression and pupils. We make space for her in our bed.

The sun at noon still flips my stomach and resurrects my sore head. An habitual Papa Bear, I fret over unpeeled fruit and mosquito bites, Bangkok air the hue of a day-old bruise. Is everyone drinking water and lathering in sun block? Is everyone, besides me, wearing a hat? Then there are my own dreams. Most sleeps they include the stone hand crooked into a *mudra*. Never can I read the gesture; never am I near to finding an answer. But our final night in the city I dream of more expansive ruins, and of stampeding elephants, their outlines in dust. Before I am quite awake I recognize this to be our immediate future, one still further away from what we have known and who we are.

In the morning my wife speaks before she is herself fully revived. "We should be getting home soon," she says. "Our parents are growing old. We should be there for them."

At breakfast I reveal a new plan. "Who wants to ride an elephant?" I say. "Ride an elephant in a city so incredible that visitors from Europe declared it the most beautiful place on earth?"

The train departs at noon.

King U-Tong established his capital of Ayutthaya in 1350 on an island at the confluence of the Chao Praya and two lesser rivers, eighty kilometres north of the Gulf of Siam. Over the next four centuries, five dynasties ruled by thirty-three monarchs widened shipping lanes and dug moats, erecting grand palaces and temples across the forty acre site. Towers called *prangs* and ceremonial tombs named *chedis* soared over the flat landscape. Rows of stone Buddhas and murals in jadeite and marble lined royal walls. Ringing the island-city was a port where silks and spices, sugar, teak and tin, were traded. Ships flying the flags of Holland, France, England and Japan moored there, alongside local barges and longboats, with awestruck sailors admiring "the sparkling towers and pyramids of the pagodas," as one French visitor described the sight. Traders constructed their own homes and embassies in the town; the Dutch even received permission to erect a cathedral, the Christian God being no threat to the Lord Buddha. "A strong great city," the Jesuit priest Abbe de Choisy called it, circa 1685. De Choisy ended his summary: "I do not know whether I have conveyed to you the impression of a beautiful view, but certainly I have never seen a lovelier."

In 1760 the Burmese King Alaungpaya attacked Ayutthaya. Though he failed to sack the capital, seven years later his son, King Hsinbyushin, laid siege once more from the far shores using cannonades and fire-boats. The city held out for fourteen months. When imperial guards finally indicated their surrender, they might have been expecting a dignified entry by Burmese victors anxious not to further damage the prize. Instead, soldiers poured onto the island bent on annihilation. Some arrived on foot and went about slaughtering towns-people and setting buildings ablaze. Others rampaged from atop squadrons of battle-elephants that crushed all in their paths. Temples and palaces were reduced to stumps and charred foundations. Icons were hacked into stubble, though not before any gold was stripped and melted down.

Thailand survived the invasion, the new capital established fur-ther south in "the village of wild olive groves," or Bangkok. But rav-aged Ayutthaya was surrendered once more, in this instance to the jungle. The latest victor enfolded the ruin in the embrace of forgetful green time: covering vines and blanketing grasses, tree roots as elabo-rate as temples.

Again, we reach the hotel at the extreme of the day's heat. Forty Celsius, a lobby thermometer reads, and no cloud cover. Still, I have to be restrained from stepping out. Ruins, especially those barely recov-ered from nature, hold a deep, primordial allure. I can go missing in them for hours without thought to my well being. Their impersonality reflects – unflatteringly, I often think – aspects of my own nature. In their magnificence and hubris, and certainly in their helplessness and pity can be found evidence of the eternal recurrence of human desires and disappointments. *We are who we are who we are,* such places confess *– until we are no longer.*

Only after I had promised elephant rides to the girls did our guidebook confirm their existence in the imperial city. In late afternoon we climb into a cab that stops at a traffic light before a bridge onto the island. The pause allows us to observe a busy modern temple where locals have gathered before a too-tall Buddha encased in a too-small chamber. Monks sit in tidy rows to one side of the statue, anonymous in their loose robes and shaved heads. Elderly women light incense sticks at the behest of the senior monk, bowing three times before the Bud-dha. Behind them, children in uniforms also bow to the idol, faces serene and black hair shiny. Anna and Claire study the children with curiosity and, perhaps, envy.

On my instructions the driver drops us a kilometre short of the ele-phant camp. To reach it, we must cross a treeless plain under a sun that bores into the skull no less viciously than it did at noon. Lured from this latest hotel pool with promises of milder air, the girls march sullenly over the grass, hats pulled low but faces still ruddy. I point out the sights – the three identical chedis of Wat Phra Sri Sanphet to the north, the conical phrang of Wat Phraram behind us – to silence. Even Mary, equally betrayed and overheated, ignores my tour guiding. In the absence of other sounds the buzz of cicadas floods the ears.

The plain is devoid of humans. No one else is foolish enough to be here. Everyone else, I think to myself – a violent, ransacking thought – has fled, or is already dead.

The camp has a roofed waiting area and a shrine to the Hindu god Ganesh, his ears festooned in garlands. Offerings of bananas and oranges gather at the deity's feet. A half-dozen real elephants wait in queue nearby, tails swishing and trunks at rest. The creatures still wear their Songkran festival tattoos. Red markings fleck the eyes and blue and pink vines cover the trunk, bracelets of leaf tangles encircling the legs. The girls select a young female with especially ornate patterns on her forehead and gold tassels off her ears. The only driver not resting, head pillowed in hands, at a table under the roof greets us. She is Belgian. "In Thailand I learn things I cannot learn anywhere else," the woman says in English.

We negotiate a forty-five minute ride and the girls climb a wooden platform that puts them on the same level as their transport. "It's like riding a boat," Claire says, once aboard. She and Anna share a wicker settee canopied by an orange umbrella. The driver is nestled on the animal's great head, snug as a monkey in a branch. "Bye-bye!" our daughters call.

"They'll be safe," I say to Mary. When I think, and then she repeats my thought out loud, the drift into waking dream – a drift I have been anticipating for days – is complete. "We're not losing them," my wife says. "Not yet."

I ask if she wants to wander the ruins with me, counting on her wishing to stay near the camp and, no doubt, keep the elephant, already a spectre out on the plain, in sight.

"Buy water," she says.

I promise.

"And wear your hat."

I promise.

"You won't wear it," she says. "Will you?"

She assures me – threatens, really – that she will wait fifteen minutes beyond the appointed time, and then will return to the hotel with her daughters. I can stay out all night if I want, with the cicadas and snakes.

A while later I collapse to the ground in Wat Phra Si Sanphet. How much of a while? I can't be sure. My watch is in my pocket, to spare it being drowned, and I lack the energy to dig it back out. Sweat likewise squirts my eyes with lime and glues my shirt to my skin. My head has split open, a hole that no baseball cap, even had I elected to keep it on, could have sealed, and various notions flow out and in. It is nice here, secluded and quiet, and I am content not to move. I am, after all, resting against a brick wall adjacent to the three-fingered hand from my dream. The chewed fingertips and severed pinkie, the gesture carved into the sandstone: there is no mistaking what is before me. Nor are the implications of finding the hand easily avoided. I last visited Ayutthaya in February 1989, for an afternoon. I doubt I saw the hand then and lodged it in my memory, to be recovered fourteen years later in Hong Kong, well in advance of deciding to flee to Thailand and then, impulsively, revisit the ruins of Old Siam. I doubt that.

This is sunstroke. This is waking dream.

The *mudra* the fingers form belongs to the Teaching Buddha. The gesture is achieved by holding the right hand in front of the chest, palm outwards, and then joining the thumb and forefinger. Teaching Buddhas lecture on the Dharma, or law, whereby ignorance and bewilderment are transformed into the wisdom of awareness. Of enlightenment.

This is not sunstroke. This is not dream.

Evening of the invasion, and Ayutthaya is engorged. Soldiers murder and plunder, their calls shrill from madness. Elephants topple houses and collapse palaces, their own cries tremulous with despair. No adult male will survive the carnage. No women or children either, it is now clear. Who am I to be witnessing the scene? A coolie filling the hulls of foreign ships or an attendant in a temple. A man with a wife and children but no name. How heavy a father's heart, knowing what will befall his dear ones. How heavy his mind, aware that he is small and useless, driven by desires and overruled by disappointments.

Scramble down to the river and find an abandoned barge. In the vessel lay the bodies of those you hold so precious, and so wished to protect, and then cast off the shore. Float out into the water. Float out to the sea. Here is now and here is how now must be. Pray to the Lord of the Lotus. Pray to be awakened.

2007

THREE FILMS ABOUT VIETNAM:

Coppola, Kubrick And War Movies

1. *Apocalypse Now* (1979)

On the flight over, a British architect summarizes the kinds of tourists who visit Danang these days. "Frenchmen rekindling colonial splendours," he says. "Plus American vets, come back to dig for MIA bones in the jungle." And what is my business in the central port city where the French first invaded Vietnam in 1858 and the U.S. marines splashed ashore in 1965? "The movies," I answer vaguely. The architect, on his way to hotel negotiations, is changing planes for Ho Chi Minh City, formerly known as Saigon.

In truth, I am a tourist as well, of still another variety. The book I am reading might betray me: *Jarhead*, Anthony Swofford's memoir of serving in the U.S. Marine Corps during the Gulf War. Swofford relates how soldiers sometimes become so agitated watching Vietnam movies that they beat each other up afterwards. "All Vietnam war films are pro-war," he writes, "no matter what their supposed message . . . . The magic brutality of the films celebrates the terrible and despicable beauty of our fighting skills."

At Danang Airfield I race through the empty terminal to admire the abandoned wartime buildings behind it. They are hulking and cavernous and could pass for a soundstage. "China Beach," I tell the taxi driver. He escorts me to a minivan without commercial markings. Concerned, I repeat the request, ignoring both that I am speaking in English and seeking a destination that persists for the most part in memory, and in movies produced seven thousand miles from here.

But the driver merely echoes my words. "China Beach," he says. "Many Americans ask for this."

I don't bother correcting him about nationality. America's war in Vietnam has made conscripts out of millions of us not quite born in-country. A showing of *Apocalypse Now* in an auditorium at the University of Toronto in the winter of 1979-80 recruited my draft-age self. It wasn't only the on-screen delirium. I also signed up for the Joseph Conrad conflict, the haunting of men by what they have witnessed and how they have behaved; the ever-darkening surface of any going-up-river tale, one bend dissolving into another, until one is truly lost and can't find a way back. Even now, a quarter-century later, I envy first-time viewers of the film. I thrill equally to news of additional battles to re-fight. *We Were Soldiers* in 2001. The 2002 re-make of *The Quiet American*, its release delayed by 9/11.

Vietnam yet bristles with cinematic urgency in the West. It is a country alive with our meanings.

The driver slows at the beach used by local people. Michael Herr's book *Dispatches* (1977) describes the "great curving stretch of beachfront" adjacent to the city of Danang, where marines were sent for R&R. "They would splash in the surf," Herr writes, "giggling and shouting, riding beach disks along the shoreline, playing like kids." Herr collaborated on the screenplays for *Apocalypse Now* and *Full Metal Jacket*. *China Beach* was a 1980s TV series about an evacuation hospital. In 2004 there is a travel company selling a tour of Vietnam, Laos and Cambodia that claims to recreate scenes from the Francis Ford Coppola film, including the sequence where soldiers are ordered by their commanding officer, Colonel Kilgore (played by Robert Duvall), to surf a strand while under enemy fire. The tour will re-enact that scene on China Beach. "Charlie Don't Surf – But You Can" the internet brochure boasts, paraphrasing Kilgore's taunt.

Finding no surfers, I provide the driver another destination. My official business here is to write about government attempts to turn that great curving stretch into a resort. Right now there is only one suitable hotel: the Furama Resort, said to be full of wistful Americans and nostalgic Frenchmen. In the Furama lobby, a Bali dream sequence of sensual comfort found at the end of a just-paved road (the hotel has been open since 1998), a Japanese customer relations woman assures me that we are on "our private China Beach." "Other beaches are not China Beach," she adds. Out on the arc, the sand as soft as brown sugar and the waves breaking into foam, I survey the emptiness, maybe thirty-kilometres of pure idyll, running north to a mountain and south to a cluster of hillocks.

Here it is, I think. And here I am, in it. The war, a little. The books, a little more. Most of all, the movies.

An elderly man renting deck chairs interrupts. He has the permanent squint and coat hanger frame of a fisherman. Surfers ride those waves, he acknowledges in French, but mostly between September and November, when the sea isn't so rough. He also mentions an undertow. To my queries about the exact location of China Beach – *the* China Beach, I emphasize, so named by geography-challenged marines – he squints first north to a place called San Teo and then south to where once there were military bases and, probably, an evacuation hospital. He gives that beach a Vietnamese name – Non Nuoc.

In the evening I wander Danang. The city is off the intrepid traveller route, which favours nearby Hue and Hoi An. A quarter-century ago some forty American facilities operated within a few kilometres of the port. Thousands of GIs must have prowled these streets, looking for beer and boom-boom. I have those scenes in my head as well, complete with Chinese lanterns and cruising cyclos, girls lingering in doorways. In a deserted hotel I order food, surrounded by employees watching a replay of a World Cup friendly – Thailand versus Malaysia – on TV. A teenaged waitress assigned to my table returns my chopsticks to their mounts if I dare rest them on my plate. Her lips are parted in shameless curiosity and her black eyes are wide.

Afterwards, I straddle sidewalks that function as outdoor restaurants, absorbing stares from diners and phonetic greetings of "hello," with mothers lifting their children up for a better look at the foreign ghost. Uncomfortable with the scrutiny, I retreat into a park. How can I be a revenant here? The beach immortalized in *Apocalypse Now*, it is true, belongs to the Philippines, while the television series was shot in Hawaii. Just about every country in southeast Asia has played Vietnam in American films, come to think of it – except for Vietnam itself. More strange, since the late 1970s there has been a curious inversion: as Americans began to make films about the war they had lost, Vietnam started forgetting, or re-contextualizing, the war it had won.

Still. This is Danang, or GI "soul city," as Michael Herr called it. This is China Beach, where Charlie Don't Surf, But You Can.

In the morning I hire a guide to sort out the beaches, and reassure myself that I am in the right cinema. Tung Lei's own story is encouraging. His father had worked for the Americans at the airfield, a job that cost him a bout in a re-education camp followed by fifteen years of unemployment. The forced idleness of the parent bequeathed to the son an intimate knowledge of wartime Danang, along with an excellent command of the English language. Tung is bright and earnest and, at just twenty-four, the breadwinner for his clan. He promises to lay out the city as it stood before he was born.

En route to the Marble Mountains, as the hillocks are called, he offers a resume of his government's campaign to halt the return of pre-1975 licentiousness. "In Danang there are the 'Five Nos,'" Tung says. "No murder, no beggars, no illiteracy, no hunger and no heroin." In Hoi An, a half-hour further south, there are three extra 'nos': no massage, no karaoke, and no women working in 'hair salons,' a popular front for brothels. He explains this with a smile, certain it is something I want to know.

So goes our tour. Tung Lei has brought me up Water Mountain, tallest of the five limestone outcrops, for a bird's-eye view of the strand. But he insists that we stop at a shrine to a female deity, where he relates a Vietnamese creation myth. One of the caverns inside the hill houses a miniature temple, complete with stone guards. Blue sky shows through gaps in the roof, courtesy, claims a sign, of American shells fired on it to flush out Vietcong. I ask about the gaps, but my guide replies with a story about Minh Mang, the emperor who lived in the palace at Hue. Minh Mang had a different wife for every day of the year. "He must have been tired," Tung says, cheeks rouging at a joke he has surely told before.

At the top of the mountain we gaze down upon a diaphanous South China Sea. Tung Lei outlines China Beach in its entirety. Below us is Non Nuoc, once home to a facility for US officers, now open ground. Further north, back towards the city, sits Bae My An, near the site of a former helicopter base. My Khe incorporates the city swimming areas, where Russian advisors frolicked during their stay, while north again, towards the foot of Monkey Mountain, are strands that he identifies only as L1 and L2. These are Vietnamese military installations. His explanations are patient and courteous, but lacking the

passion he shows for emperors and deities and government efforts to
elevate morals. It is as though he has never quite grasped my request
for a war tour, or else hasn't an inkling about how films can overrun a
person, like a small country by a larger one.

I decide to name names. "A-pock-lips?" Tung says of the one
movie that might help him appreciate my interest. In the backpacker
district of Ho Chi Minh City they sell T-shirts emblazoned with the film
title. Yet here, near the source of that particular up-the-river tale, a local
has never heard of it? He inquires about the term. "A kind of prophesy," I answer with an emotion close to regret. "Usually of doom and
destruction."

2. *Full Metal Jacket* (1987)

A cyclo driver is hawking a tour of the old capital. He pedals along the
curb while I straddle the sidewalk, on my way to a trophy display of
war detritus. Tanks bearing unit numbers on their shells, Hueys fire-
gutted and skeletal, along with insect-shaped artillery weapons, bar-
rels aimed at the sky, rust on a lawn. Behind the display are elegant traditional buildings, presently used as museums; adjacent is the north
wall of the Imperial Enclosure. It houses the Forbidden Purple City,
former residence of emperors. These walls, like the walls of the Imperial Enclosure itself – ten kilometres of city-fortress, encased in a moat –
are pockmarked and scarred, as if from a bout of smallpox, once a
feared assassin of Asian royalty.

This is Hue, a nearly religious site for Vietnamese. Until 1968 the
city's imperial splendours, by then largely architectural, spared it being
enlisted as a battleground. The Tet Offensive cancelled the privilege. In
January of that year the Vietcong stealthily crossed its bridges and
occupied the citadel. At the end of the month the American marines, in
company with the South Vietnamese army, resolved to take the town
back. The battle lasted twenty-six days, leaving ten thousand residents
dead.

"You are interested in the war?" the cyclo driver asks. Thinking
ruefully of Danang, I hesitate. My plan now is to revert to guidebook
tourism, to visit the Imperial Museum and the Halls of the Mandarins,

the Royal Library and Nine Holy Cannons. Later on I'll head out to the tombs south of the city, including the one for Minh Mang, which most visitors reach by riding a ferry across the Perfume River. My book describes it as "majestic."

But last week I happened to watch *Full Metal Jacket* again for the first time in a decade. Earlier today I found myself scouring the outskirts of Hue for the industrial wastelands that host the film's battle sequences. I kept a look out for the intersection where Private Joker, the anti-hero, banters with a prostitute. (She has virtually the script's only lines of dialogue by a Vietnamese. *Apocalypse Now* offers locals even less of a say.) I sought the drab buildings where the marines get cut down by a wily and methodical sniper, who proves to be a teenage girl. The final sequence in the film follows the marines as they hunt and eventually kill this enemy.

My eyes sought a parallel in reality despite knowing that *Full Metal Jacket* was filmed in England. Stanley Kubrick did not care for travel, and instead spent millions first recreating the city of Hue, and then re-destroying it, in a dockyard outside London. "We worked from still photographs of Hue in 1968," the director explained. "Now, not every bit of it was right, but some of the buildings were absolute carbon copies of the outer industrial areas . . . We had demolition guys in there for a week, laying charges . . . Then we had a wrecking ball there for two months, with the art director telling the operator which hole to knock in which building . . . All in all," Kubrick concluded, "a tremendous set dressing and rubble job."

"You were here during the fighting?" I finally answer the cyclo driver.

"I was a boy," he says. "Eight years old. Our house near gate where Americans enter. My whole life, I live in Hue."

Dismounting, the man introduces himself simply as Tran. Tran's hair is dishevelled and his shirt-collar is frayed. His pants are tied using a length of rope. His gaze, though, is clear and warm and his handshake is firm. He tips the seat forward for me to climb into, his flip-flops clacking. Tran says he is forty-three, with a wife and two children. I, coincidentally, am the same.

Cyclos, or pedicabs, put the passenger seat before the rider, rendering eye contact difficult. For much of the hour-long tour my guide is a voice in my ear and a mild smell of cigarettes in my nostrils. Unlike Tung Lei in Danang, Tran knows exactly what I am seeking. He documents the Battle of Hue that he experienced in February 1968, a boy elated and terrified through days of mortar fire and flames and nights of sirens and smoke. He indicates where he and his friends followed marines up an alley – the soldiers had heavy boots and big behinds – in search of Vietcong. He pedals out a causeway in Tinh Tam Lake to detail a sniper exchange he tried to sneak a look at, narrowly missing a bullet. Tran also points down a road where he joined a frantic effort to clear the floor of a bombed house. They found a baby beneath a collapsed wall, its cheeks blue.

"No school for a month," he says. "A strange holiday."

Then his own house was shelled, his sister and grandmother killed. There was also an uncle executed by the Vietcong during their occupation. Later, city dwellers unearthed the mass graves of "collaborators." Those deaths aren't much talked about; the Vietcong eventually won the war, and became their liberators.

"And your parents?" I have to ask.

He halts the cyclo in a neighbourhood of detached homes. I step down from my perch so we can talk beneath a small pagoda, its upper floor converted into a pillbox for soldiers or police. Kids kick a soccer ball near us.

Tran removes a photo from his pocket. Though cracked and creased, the face of a man in the uniform of the South Vietnamese army is still visible. The resemblance between father and son isn't striking; it is disconcerting, an abrupt collapse less of time than distance, as if what was up on a screen is now down off it, smiling and watching me admire his image, captured by a camera.

"Your father?" I say stupidly.

The quaver in his reply is impossible to ignore.

"He was away from Hue during battle," he answers. "He die fighting in DMZ in 1972."

"You look like him."

"I miss him very much," he says, lowering his gaze. He touches the top of the photo with his fingertip, as if to re-assure his parent of his enduring regard, but does not demand its return. I hand it back anyway.

When a ball bounces off the cab my guide exchanges words with the boys. I use the pretext to ask if the children are aware the nicks in the wall behind us are from gunfire, or that soldiers likely died in the pillbox over our heads.

His voice drops to the whisper he used when recounting his uncle's execution. "Only a little," he says. After 1975, war memories became sanctioned and censored, credible only if they validated the victors. And who is Tran to inform these youngsters about their own history? He is a cyclo driver because his father wore the wrong uniform. He holds up his pants with rope.

He tells his daughter much of what he has told me, he confesses, though not everything. She has the top grades in her class, and may qualify for a spot at university. He is teaching her the English he learned before unification, to help her succeed. His ten-year-old son is interested only in soccer and video games.

We shake hands again. It doesn't even occur to me to ask if he has heard of a movie named after a superior brand of bullet, one designed not to fragment inside its target, and which was filmed in various locations, including an abandoned dockyard outside London. This is Hue, and he has lived here his entire life.

3. *The Quiet American* (remake, 2002)

In Hoi An I stroll to the river at sunset, easy in my stride. The evening – and my head – will be free of cinema. The town is too dreamy, too much a wishful reverie of antiquity, to conjure curved beaches or industrial wastelands. Streets of pagodas and assembly halls wind down to a riverside lined with boats. Shops sell silk slippers and traditional dresses, the *au dia*, tailored for tourists in an afternoon. I will hire no guide and ask no locals about their lives. *Jarhead* has been left back at my hotel, replaced by a novel set in New York.

But then, emerging near a footbridge, I squint in recognition of the setting. Assuming it to be from a photograph – I have never been in Hoi An before – I cross the bridge, remarking on the absence of lanterns along the famous covered bridge fifty metres farther up river. Again, I wonder why I would expect these decorations. I am seated on the terrace of a restaurant off the landing when, once more, my eye insists. This time, it provides details. An older man is crossing the footbridge at night, a lantern-lit arch behind him. He is being escorted to a table in a café, where he can watch for the friend he has just betrayed.

Thomas Fowler, as played by Michael Caine. The Daikow Bridge in Saigon, as re-created in Hoi An. The penultimate scene in *The Quiet American*, no less, with Fowler waiting to dine with the agent Alden Pyle (Brendan Fraser) in Cholon, Saigon's Chinatown, once the most notorious neighbourhood in the country, rife with brothels and opium dens and "taxi girls" on the prowl. The apotheosis of smoky, decadent Asia, as filtered through the lens of Graham Greene. Greene, of course, was a movie fan.

An elderly waitress serves me a beer. "Was there? . . ." I begin to say, indicating the footbridge. My tone is apologetic.

"Mr Michael Caine," she answers.

"Really?"

"Make movie here in Hoi An!"

Her pride confuses me until I recall a magazine article extolling Phillip Noyce's remake of the original 1958 adaptation as one of the first western films to receive permission to shoot inside Vietnam.

A young English couple order food at the next table. The man flips through a pirated copy of *The Quiet American*. "Fowler is having second thoughts about letting Pyle be assassinated," he says to his companion. "He crosses back over the bridge there, hoping to intervene."

"Caine was brilliant, don't you think?" the woman says.

"He was ten years too old for the part."

"Brendan Fraser didn't seem, I don't know, American enough," she says.

Though I feign reading my book, my thoughts have already joined the conversation. Brendan Fraser was terrific as Pyle, I counter silently, capturing how certain men bury their ambition and zeal in excess amiability and the body language of a teenager.

Soon the couple are running through the list. *Apocalypse Now* is the consensus masterpiece. Both remember the Russian roulette scene in *The Deer Hunter* and Jon Voight's performance in *Coming Home*. ("Who walks into the ocean at the end?" she asks. "Bruce Dern," he answers.) The man hated *Casualties of War*, which the woman hasn't seen. He appreciates the boot camp sequences in *Full Metal Jacket,* and thinks Kubrick was a more perceptive critic of the war than Coppola. She wonders about Oliver Stone's *Platoon,* which he can't recall very well, except the ending.

"*Platoon* is too didactic," I say out loud.

The man smiles. We exchange greetings.

"The first Vietnam film I ever saw was called *The Losers,*" I continue, "at a drive-in outside Toronto. It was an insanely violent story about bikers who get recruited by the CIA to rescue a politician kidnapped in Cambodia, and all wind up dead. I was maybe twelve, and had never seen anything like it. I still remember one scene . . ."

We talk movies for two hours, ordering more food and beer from the waitress, whose face I barely register and whose excitement over the appearance of Michael Caine in her town I neglect to further query, mindful, perhaps, that her comments would likely drift into a sorrowful account of her own life. Our manner is relaxed and intimate, as though we are old friends, typical of the encounters one has while travelling in foreign countries, and of the effect chatting about films has on people. Night darkens beyond the terrace, and lanterns are indeed lit along the riverbank. It's a charming effect, one I have to believe is for our benefit.

2005

SHANGHAI BEAUTY:

On Being Small In China

Wang Gangfeng is a happy man. He tells me as much one afternoon in Shanghai. The photographer sits in his studio in the city's west end. The studio occupies an upper-floor corner of a defunct work unit residence, and in its day may have housed a dozen families in the forced intimacy for which China, and especially Shanghai, remains notorious. Now Wang, a boyish fifty-two-year-old attired in all-black, including leather pants and boots, has the space to himself. Appropriately, he is equally the self-stylized "first freelance photographer in China" and proprietor of the "Gang of One," a business name drawn from a pun on the infamous Gang of Four clique that reigned terror on China in the 1970s.

His walls are as crowded as any city block. Though Wang earns his living doing commercial work, his art lies in the portrait photography that shirks neither Shanghai grit nor rural backwardness. Images include elderly ladies in alleyways and bicyclists pushing impossible loads. His lens is intimate, and with even the most impersonal shots, including a well-known photo of a solitary biker parting a sea of fellow travellers heading the opposite direction, the eye is drawn to the often serene expressions worn by those going about their arduous business.

It is a pleasure to meet Wang Gangfeng again after many years. I am back in Shanghai to talk to locals about the transformation of their city into both a twenty-first century colossus and – in the views of certain critics – an emblem of urban living at its most sterile and inhuman. Wang's thinking, like his photography, reflects a sensibility particular to certain Chinese, one characterized by an elasticity of thought which seeks to reconcile the grand with the intimate, public necessity with private destiny. Such thinking may be how the individual in China best negotiates various powerful impulses within the culture, especially tendencies towards the gargantuan. It may also be how he or she both

71

survives them, and finds a kind of beauty and self-esteem in the land-scape they must inhabit.

Wang, who returned to China from a self-imposed exile in Canada in 1995, says of the new Shanghai, "I am very happy to witness this period of history." He likens the period to nothing less monumental than the Industrial Revolution in Europe and the Gold Rush in America. But his observations about the upheaval, which has seen the city expand both horizontally and vertically beyond even the most fevered of central committee imaginings – as well as across the Huangpu River in the form of Pudong, a mirror of Shanghai that literally did not exist two decades ago – aren't those of an urban planner, aloof from the consequences of his grand schemes.

In the 1990s, Wang's parents were among the hundreds of thousands of Shanghainese displaced by the erasure of entire neighbourhoods for re-development as high-rise and commercial zones, or else to allow for the expressways that now lattice the city. His family wound up content with their replacement dwelling in an outlying suburb, but only after much anxiety, financial and otherwise. The photographer is also a defender of the few remaining *shikumen*, the traditional red-brick neighbourhoods whose destruction has become almost a visual cliché for heedless progress. Of the ten Shanghai photos in his book *China*, for instance, Canadian photographer Edward Burtynsky includes no fewer than seven images featuring destroyed, or partially destroyed, housing units. For his part, Wang Gangfeng gives walking tours of the *shikumen* where he was raised, mostly for curious foreigners.

His own apartment, however, where he lives with his wife and young daughter, is in a new building, and he is stoic about local ambivalence towards these reminders of pre-transformed Shanghai. "My neighbours and friends don't see anything special in the old houses," he says. "Either they want modern apartments or else they are tired of history." What about the cultural loss once the final *shikumen* is bull-dozed? "We are going to lose the character of these neighbourhoods," Wang answers. "But that's the only thing we are losing. And we are gaining much more."

The gain, simply, is dignified living conditions. Dignified, as in indoor plumbing, and individual kitchens, privacy from the neighbours. "It's a completely different world now," Wang says of Shanghai in 2006. Soaring prosperity – the city has a per capita income five times the national average – is, in turn, forging more empowered homeowners, an evolution that has already begun to slow the runaway train of development. For Wang Gangfeng, this easing up is likewise part of the grand scheme. "Shanghai has been a construction site for many years," he says, his thinking once more stretching out. "But now it is almost finished." He even provides a date: the World Fair in 2010. "The city will be completed by then," he adds with a smile.

The ongoing project that is Shanghai leaves many observers uneasy, especially Westerners. Asian cities, from Bangkok to Manila to Saigon, share similar caffeinated lifestyles and organizational impulses with their Chinese counterparts, along with the same urgent needs of rapidly urbanizing populations. Visitors from the West, whose own cities seem church-hushed by comparison, are more awed and, often enough, disconcerted by such places. They also tend to be judgemental, summoning visions of the future cityscapes that await us all, dystopias of disorder and environmental meltdown evidenced by flickering neon and smoke rising from grates. A generation ago it was the Tokyo of William Gibson's *Neuromancer* that induced these anxieties. Today it appears to be Shanghai.

Scale is what probably unsettles the most. The city is impossible to absorb in a single visual sweep. It seems, moreover, twice as distended as in 2001, the time of my last visit, and about twice that again from when I first negotiated an endless terrain of construction cranes and building sites back in 1997. (A preliminary experience, in 1989, belonged to another era, when Shanghai, still being punished by the central government for its pre-communist decadence and Cultural Revolution fanaticism, wore the rags and coal-grime of a Dickens urchin, its beleaguered residents squeezed into a space designed for a third their number.) Every few years, a major new skyline sprouts from the marshy Yangtze basin. Over there is New York, replicated in central Pudong. Further down is Toronto, stretched along the river south of the inner core. The entirety of Montreal is visible from the front steps of the Shanghai Museum, facing north. Turn south, and Vancouver suddenly materializes. West of People's

Square one sees all of Chicago, with Milwaukee thrown in for good measure. On rare haze-free days, visible to the west, south and north are further office towers and high-rises – the assembled city vistas of Texas, say.

Edward Burtynsky's images trail me around this megalopolis for three days. Once viewed, his extraordinary panoramas of Shanghai, often taken from on high and favouring the raw evidence of urban renewal, are difficult to erase from memory. Shanghai, which he has described as "capitalism on steroids," comes across as monstrous, a chimera out of control. It has no shape, except for its bloated size, and seems without character. Most tellingly, the ten Shanghai pictures in *China* are devoid of people, aside from a few tiny figures scurrying amongst the rubble. A city of twenty million and counting, and scarcely anyone is around.

Burtynsky's subject, of course, is not the citizens of Shanghai. His interest lies in physical settings. He takes photographs of how human endeavours and actions have transformed – and generally devastated – nature, and his starting point for China, as he explains in his artist statement to the book, is how the country is "the most recent participant to be seduced by western ideals – the hollow promise of fulfillment and happiness through material gain." A passionate environmentalist, Burtynsky won't be dissuaded by any arguments for exceptional Chinese circumstances. "I no longer see my world as delineated by countries, with borders, or language, but as 6.5 billion humans living off a precariously balanced, finite planet," he writes.

Exhibitions of Edward Burtynsky's China photographs, most notably his images of the Three Gorges Dam and various labour-intensive industries, where uniformed workers are shown head-bowed and anonymous, draw near chorus-like public and media responses in the West. We find his China cold and foreboding, "an Orwellian universe of strictly regulated collective effort that is unimaginable, and – to my mind at least – it's scary," as one Canadian newspaper critic expressed it.

I put the Burtynsky vision of Shanghai to Edward Denison and Guangyu Ren. We are in a bar on the seventh floor of a 1920s building along the Bund, the historic downtown once considered the paradigm of westernized Asian architecture. Denison and Ren are co-authors of

Building Shanghai: The Story of China's Gateway, a strident reading of the city's past, present, and future. He is an ex-patriot English design consultant and photographer; she is an architect, born and raised in Shanghai and educated in England and Australia. A married couple, they are bi-racial and bi-cultural and soon to be parents. "The Buck Rogers scenario goes back to the early twentieth century," Edward Denison explains. "Shanghainese have always had to live in the shadows of their skyscrapers." In the late 1920s alone, Denison adds, some 12,000 buildings were torn down and replaced by taller and more formidable structures. "There was talk then about how Shanghai was being destroyed."

Though the authors are critical of the current transformation, change, massive and mostly callous, has forever been the fuel for Shanghai's engine, and citizens have had no choice but to adapt. An acceptance of change, along with a capacity to thrive under it, may even define that notoriously vigorous character. "It's the same now as it was a hundred years ago. Poor people are always coming in from the countryside to earn a living. They open small shops or sell their vegetables on street corners. That's not going to change," says Ren with a nod to the rough resiliency of the people. Westerners, Denison remarks, vacillate between nostalgia for those colonial buildings, such as the one we're in – "They look cozy to the western eye," he remarks – and dismay at the "sci-fi" city of today. But Shanghai has never been the sum of its vaulting and over-reaching architectural ambitions. It is the sum of its streets, and of the lives lived, in effect, at street-eye level. "Streets too crowded," Ren Guangyu says, listing the century-old complaints, "can't walk on the pavement. Too many people, too little space!" She and Denison recently bought an apartment here.

That evening, I page through *Building Shanghai* in my room at the Metrople Hotel, a gloomy, Gotham-like 1930 edifice that might well have engendered a few brooding visitor prophesies in its day. But 1930 was already late to the whither-Shanghai business. In 1866, a certain P.G. Laurie declared this about the future: "Shanghai is undoubtedly a great ruin. Like many young and rising aspirants it has been carried away by the magnificence of its prospects." In 1901, the British author J. Ricalton experienced the coming apocalypse first-hand: the old town, he said, "is traversed by lanes or streets that might better be termed fetid tunnels . . . Odours are suffocating and the eyes can find nothing attractive or beautiful to rest upon: squalor, indigence, misery, slush, stench, depravity, dilapidation, and decay prevail everywhere." Further along, a 1916 travelogue by Mary Ninde Gamewell foresaw doom for impudent Shanghai: "Changes are going on continually all over the city," she wrote. "Day by day old buildings are disappearing and modern ones rising in their place. It is to be feared that many of the ancient landmarks will soon be gone."

Clearly, I am wrong to lay only globalized twenty-first century Western anxieties at the foot of Shanghai. Viewed from on high, and likely in passing, this has always been a scary and upsetting city.

Southern Beauty, a restaurant in the former French Concession, is entranced through a watery dream. Slanted walls of running water bracket an elevated path along a corridor. A mirror door at the end slides opens when approached. Inside the dining room, I am shown to a table next to a floor-to-ceiling glass window looking onto the street. My lunch companion, a vivacious twenty-nine-year-old lawyer named Zhen Feng, is already seated. She is tiny and tidy and wears a cream-coloured business suit and a warm smile. After shaking hands we exchange business cards, Feng's emerging from a slim silver case. A waiter pours tea and we sit for a minute, admiring the surroundings.

My opening comment describes the serenity not so much of the restaurant, which weds Eastern service to Western prices, as the sidewalk beyond the window. Previous strolls of the narrow laneways involved negotiating – to paraphrase Ren Guangyu – too little space with too many locals in too great a hurry. Today, at least, the streets of Shanghai are easy, and even pleasing, to walk.

"Shanghai is more liveable now than it was ten years ago," Zhen says. "It is also more likeable." A native of Xiamen in Fujian province, she views the city with both the elasticity of Wang Gangfeng and the scepticism of a provincial, raised on tales of the chaotic metropolis and its all-elbows citizenry. But she, too, has remarked on the dwindling of those sidewalk scrums and pitch-battles to board public buses. "No question, the quality of life has improved," she says. "It isn't only on the material side, either. Shanghai is cleaner. People are more polite."

Like everyone else I speak with, Zhen Feng acknowledges the harshness with which the improvements have been achieved, especially the destruction of traditional dwellings and the relocation of their residents. Yet she also insists that "the government now has better skills at building a city." And a better designed city makes everyone calmer. "If the rules are reasonable, people will follow them," she says. Prosperity, too, is serving to improve Shanghai, and the incessant bulging of the municipal seams with newcomers is fine by her. "It is part of the dynamism," she says.

When it comes to living in Shanghai, the issue of enormity is simply not a factor. "It has always been too big," Zhen says, echoing Ren. Though her husband is currently back in Xiamen, where he owns a business, she has no problem envisioning raising a family here. She hopes to buy an apartment on her salary as a lawyer for an international firm. A globalized person herself – she recently completed further training in the United States – Zhen Feng plans to send her own children to a Shanghai school where both Mandarin and English are taught.

On the third floor of the Shanghai Urban Planning Museum is the now famous vast scale model of the urban area as it should look in 2020. As outsized and surreal as the city itself, the model is popular with locals, who encircle the waist-high projection on elevated walkways seeking out their present or perhaps future living quarters, often exclaiming in delight when they locate a plastic facsimile of their apartment. The exhibit has proven such a hit that a smaller version – a model of the model of the reality outside the front doors – has been constructed in the lobby below.

While metafictionist Italo Calvino would have enjoyed the museum, its natural literary analogue may be Jonathan Swift's *Gulliver's Travels*. The model allows Shanghainese to strut like the oversized Gulliver among Lilliputians for a few moments, before stepping back into the land of the Brobdingnags, where they are once more tiny and helpless. Unless, that is, those people don't consider themselves as being either one size or the other. In *Gulliver's Travels*, whose subtitle "Travels into Several Remote Nations" was understood by eighteenth-century readers to refer to the Far East, Brobdingnags appear grotesque for the simple reason that their huge dimensions magnify what are otherwise ordinary human flaws. "Nothing is great or little otherwise than by comparison," Swift writes of this perceptual irony.

Many Chinese may well feel dwarfed by their mammoth nation, including its still massive inequalities and the use of coercion and control to keep its citizens in step. Many will certainly share Edward Burtynsky's concern about how the development of China – a pattern of growth that will see as many as 400 million additional people pour into the cities in the next couple of decades, all seeking better material lives – will impact on their environment, and the planet as a whole.

But any country that built the Great Wall and the Grand Canal probably isn't going to find the Three Gorges Dam, or the transformation of Shanghai, especially daunting. Likewise, residents of that nation, accustomed to social engineering on a scale at once mythic and commiserate with real needs, may accept and even take pride in developments that outsiders view as distressing. What is missing in Burtynsky's China are its people; what defines Wang Gangfeng's photos are the individuals he sees everywhere. What defines Burtynsky's Shanghai, in turn, is destruction and sterility, nearly the opposite impression Zhen Feng gives of the town where she happily works, eats and lives, at street level.

If anything, Wang and Zhen are both asserting, using different vocabularies, the re-emergence of the private self, after decades of ideology-imposed sublimation. But to do that, the self must be reconciled with the non-self of collective, and generally colossal, endeavour, once the exclusive state-approved narrative of socialist China. Taking the next step, towards finding aspects of all this – the sprawl, the enterprise, even the spasms of heedless progress and degradation – somehow beautiful, isn't such a leap. It's your own life, isn't it, in your ever-transforming, if still stolidly oppressive, society? Why shouldn't you feel good about how well some things are going?

At a show of Edward Burtynsky's China photos in Toronto last year, guests were invited to record their thoughts in a notebook. Most offered remarks praising the work and sharing its presumed critique of the subject, using words like 'disquieting' and 'upsetting.' But one entry was written in pin-yin, the westernized form of Mandarin, and signed by someone with a Chinese name. "Such beautiful pictures!" the visitor proclaimed. That particular guest wasn't looking at different photos. He or she must just be seeing things differently.

2006

PROSE

LINGUA FRANCHISE:

English The Conqueror

In a restaurant in Singapore's Little India district I chatted recently with a man doling out bowls of fishhead curry. He called me a "mat saleh," Malay for 'white foreigner.' He also dubbed a woman who walked past us an "S.P.G." – a 'Sarong Party Girl.' According to him, uppercrust Singaporians who put on posh accents were "chiak kantang." "Chiak" is Hokkien for 'eating,' "kantang" a mangling of the Malay for 'potatoes.' 'Eating potatoes': affecting Western mannerisms.

Singapore has four official languages: Mandarin, English, Malay, and Tamil. But at street level there is no mother tongue. Except for among older Chinese, who still speak the Hokkien dialect, the city-state's *lingua franca* is actually Singlish, a much-loved, much-frowned-upon hodgepodge of languages and slang. When the man in the restaurant asked if I could pay with a smaller bill, he expressed it this way: "Got, lah?" I recognized that bit of cobbling. In Hong Kong, where I was then living, Cantonese speakers sprinkle their English with similar punctuation. "Lah" often denotes a question, like "eh" for Canadians. "Wah" infers astonishment.

Once, walking through that city's nightclub district with a Chinese friend, we nearly knocked into a Canto-pop star, a young man of smouldering Elvis looks. "Wah, now can die!" my friend said, only half-jokingly.

If English is the region's compromise tongue, default neutral terrain for doing deals and making friends, loan words and hybrid street dialects serve to advance its utility. It is the same across most of Asia. In the Philippines, Tagalog speakers refer to a look-alike as a "Xerox" and an outdated fad as a "chapter." "Golets," they say, meaning 'Let's go.' Anything first-rate in Bombay gets called "cheese," from 'chiz,' the Hindi word for 'object.' In Japan, students on a Friday night announce "Let's beer!" and salarymen quit smoking because of a "dokutosutoppu," a 'doctor-stop,' or orders from their physician. The majority of these word constructions would be no more comprehensible to a North American than the latest slang out of England or Australia. They belong to the places that mouthed them.

All this activity marks an interesting point from which to examine the latest evidence surrounding the explosion of English, which now boasts 1.9 billion competent speakers worldwide. In the view of Montreal writer Mark Abley, author of *Spoken Here: Travels Among Threatened Languages*, "no other language has ever enjoyed the political, economic, cultural, and military power that now accompanies English." English, he says, acts like a "brand name" and serves as a "repository of global ambition." Describing a quiz given to young Malaysians that contained references to American culture, Abley reports: "The obvious theme is the United States. But the subtler theme, I think, is power."

"Language annihilation," he writes, may just be one battle in the "wider war" – "the fight to sustain diversity on a planet where globalizing, assimilating, and eradicating occur on a massive scale." Mark Abley is far from alone in linking the spread of English with fears of a bland consumerist empire – i.e. with a certain vision of American might. Geoffrey Hull, an Australian linguist quoted in *Spoken Here*, advises the banning of unsubtitled English programming on TV in East Timor. "English," Hull warns, "is a killer language."

Such unease isn't hard to understand. Of the 6,000 living languages, some ninety percent are at risk of vanishing before the end of this century. These are tongues spoken by fewer than 100,000 people, and rarely as the only means of communication. For certain linguists, the death of each marks the disappearance of a world view. Without a language to call one's own, original stories stop being told and unique conversations with God diminish. English triumphs just one set of stories and one conversation.

But is the link between the "tidal wave" of English, as Abley describes it, and the threat to variety so direct? History isn't without precedents for this kind of upheaval. With a few centuries of the empire in Ancient Greece, for instance, languages spoken by Trojans, Sumerians, Lydians, Etruscans and Scythians, had been rendered extinct. Each of those societies contributed to the first great renaissance in

western civilization. Classical Greek itself went on to serve as a foundation for a few other languages, including this one.

Cries of English the cultural barbarian aren't new, either. In the
19th century, France's *civilisatrice* and Germany's *kultur* programs
granted the colonial aggressions of those nations a patina of benevo-
lence. England's ambitions, in contrast, were given no similar benefit of
the doubt, being equated from the start with an unbridled lust for
power. Over the past fifty years, as the U.S. has come to supplant Cruel
Britannia as the primary 'exporter' of the tongue, it has had to bear
most of the criticisms. When a Muslim group recently denounced the
Arabic version of the *Idol* TV series because it "facilitates the culture of
globalization led by America," it didn't matter that the program had
originated in England. In certain minds, English can only ever be the
language of McDonald's and Nike, Madonna and Cruise.

By such reasoning, English couldn't form a natural part of
Singaporian street life or Filipino cross-language talk. It couldn't be the
rightful possession of the millions of Indians who now call it their
mother tongue. But the truth is, English isn't just exploding across the
universe; it is being exploded on contact with other societies and languages. No single political power or region, it could be argued, can
fairly claim it as its exclusive spokesperson.

In Asia, at least, English feels this protean. The Hong Kong author
Nury Vittachi has been charting the emergence of a pan–Southeast-
Asian argot. He calls the argot 'Englasian,' the wonky dialect of international business types and youthful hipsters. Vittachi even penned a
short play in Englasian titled *Don't Stupid Lah, Brudder*. The setting is a
bar in a Jakarta hotel and the characters are a Malaysian investor, an
Indian accountant, and an Australian entrepreneur. The Malay says
things like "No nid-lah, sit-sit, don't shy." The Auzzie counters with
"Don't do yer lolly, mate. Let's have a squiz." Of the three, the Indian is
the most readily intelligible. She speaks of how she might be able to
"facilitate my cousin-brother, a revered Sydneysider."

Spend any time in the region and two things become obvious.
First, English still makes only a minor noise, and only in the major cities. Its consumer blandishments pale against homegrown magazines,
movies, and pop singers. No major Asian language, be it Mandarin,
Malay, Japanese, or any of the fourteen principal Indian tongues, is at

risk of vanishing. Interestingly, those languages are themselves killing off their own sub-dialects and non-standard variants. The world is everywhere too connected for the health of the linguistically vulnerable.

The second observation relates to the playfulness of inventions like Singlish. If Asians are threatened by the growing presence of English, they are expressing their fear in the strangest manner – by inviting the danger into their homes. Linguists praise a language for its capacity to acquire and assimilate expressions from elsewhere. Such openness is taken as a sign of confidence and growth. The principal languages of nearly half of humanity are, by this measure, prospering. English isn't storming these cultures to wage war on them. The locals certainly aren't under that impression. They view the language mostly as a tool, one they can manipulate, and even call their own.

2003

DUMB AS A SACK OF HAMMERS:

A Southern Ontario Childhood

To prepare for an interview with Roddy Doyle a few years ago, I invited an Irish journalist living in Canada for a drink. We were discussing the riotous take on working-class Dublin speech found in Doyle's Barrytown trilogy of novels, and I mentioned the joke from *The Van* where a customer approaches the fast food truck and orders a "Dunphy and chips," instead of the regular sausage. The customer isn't asking for anything new. Rather, he has renamed the tube-of-meat a 'Dunphy,' in mocking honour of sports analyst Eamon Dunphy, whose sour commentaries on the Irish soccer team were outraging fans during the fevered weeks of the 1990 World Cup. A Dunphy, then, was a sausage-shaped blowhard; a Dunphy was a prick. From my years in Ireland I knew such neologisms to be routine, born of a delight in verbal energy and excess – talk as entertainment, even as self-expression. It was easy to envision Roddy Doyle's slight leaping from the pages of fiction into the pubs and street corners of the society that encouraged such invention.

The journalist agreed. But then he flipped the observation. Could such a thing ever happen in Canada? he asked. Take our own very own enervating sports commentator, hockey analyst Don Cherry. He seemed resident in the Canadian equivalent of Barrytown. He was certainly ripe for being canonized as a verb or noun. "Don't go all Don Cherry on me" for an explosion of flag waving, shaded by xenophobia. "There's a real Cherry" for a hockey puck malapropism. Here was a perfect chance for Canadian speech to assert itself: show some liveliness, be playful and alert and alive to event and circumstance. Here was a chance for us to prove that we, too, can have our linguistic fun.

Or not.

The Irishman lamented how Canadians treat the English language. We like our speech buttoned and starched and ironed stiff. Valuing neither invention nor recklessness, we get all shirty at the hint of extravagance or excess. Plain donuts only, please, and a double-double coffee, thank you very much. There were, we agreed, exceptions. The brilliant dialects of Newfoundland were the obvious holdout, along with those pockets of old-time Nova Scotia and Prince Edward Island where television had yet to regularize accents and obliterate idioms. As a sidebar – our complaint applied only to the English-speaking country – I noted the thriving linguistic energy of Québecois French. An example came to mind. Early in his career the reclusive novelist Réjean Ducharme received credit for the neologism "ma blonde," a term for a girlfriend or even long-term companion that entered the lexicon of Quebec street speech almost overnight. But Ducharme's creativity has continued unabated. In his latest novel, Dévadé, the signature sound of Kellog's Rice Krispies cereal, "snap, crackle, pop" is rendered into French as "*le cric croc.*" The main character takes this linguistic oddity, a combination of an anglicism and child's verbal play, and transforms it into an absurdist vocable -- "*que le cric me croc.*" Meaning: "How the snap crackles my pop."

The mention of Ducharme shifted our focus to writers and writing. Without prompting, the journalist launched into a wider complaint about the almost wilful linguistic dullness of most Canadian writers, including the majority of our icons. No surprise to him, at least, nearly all the guilty hailed from flat-tongued Ontario. Southern Ontario, to be more exact: Anglo-Saxon Toronto, and its broad cultural and spiritual environs. Robertson Davies and Margaret Atwood, Alice Munro and Timothy Findley, Jane Urquhart and Barbara Gowdy, all shared prose styles that, notwithstanding their elegance and charged poetry, displayed little to nil impulse to unbutton and dress down on the page. They were grammatically preservative and idiomatically conservative. They had no ear to any local ground. In the view of the Irishman, such class and place neutral prose situated too many leading Canadian authors in the linguistically joyless and tone-deaf demographic neighbourhood known as the North American middleclass, where lively language apparently came to die.

His attack put me on the defensive. Maybe Canadian speech, and much Canadian prose, wasn't as dynamic as in Ireland or as dishevelled as in Scotland. Maybe it lacked the laconic charm of certain regions in the southern United States. But weren't we a new society, still evolving our identity, language and otherwise? Australia was newer than Canada, the journalist fired back, and it was a linguistic free-for-all, besotted with invention. Same went for the coursing dialects of the Caribbean. Could I name another country where English had been spoken for so long, and from such a stance of political security, and still managed to remain so simpering and bland?

I went home and examined a novel I had just finished. Feeling plucky, I had a character who is walking along a street in Montreal in January, and can't breathe for the cold, announce that it was "truly Lord Franklin out this afternoon," referring to the 19th-century British explorer whose expedition expired in the Arctic. A small gesture, I thought. A step out of that linguistic suburb. The manuscript came back from the copy editor with two queries about the "Lord Franklin" allusion. First, the editor informed me that, contrary to popular lore, John Franklin was only a "Sir," never a "Lord." Second, was I trying to suggest it was really cold out that day and, if so, why didn't I just say as much?

I come from the heart – or the hole – of plain donut Canadian speech. The post-war Willowdale street where I was born in 1960 featured rows of boxy bungalows and A-frames and equally straight lines of talk and behaviour. Inhabited, for the most part, by lower-middle-class Anglo-Saxons, it was a place where Italian food meant macaroni and cheese and breaded chicken balls conjured the mysteries of the Orient. Paul Anka was a nice boy from nice Ottawa, Pierre Trudeau a dangerous but interesting man from distant, foreign-tongued Quebec. Houses flapped the Union Jack from backyard poles. Bagpipes rang out on Saturday mornings, agitating squirrels. Our neighbour on one side was a garbage man named Billy. A bachelor with an easy grin but irregular teeth, Billy wore bristly cheek growth and permanently stained overalls. Our properties shared a driveway, and Billy always greeted me with a friendly "How're you doing, kid?" – and nothing more. On the other side were a Scots-Presbyterian clan called the MacGregors. They said nothing, literally, to our family; the parents had seemingly forbidden their four daughters contact with neighbourhood children, fearful, perhaps, of our capacities for speech at all.

Contact between neighbours on Dunview Avenue, between those cramped homes and trim yards, was ruled by WASP house rules. Good fences didn't make good neighbours in this Toronto; no real conversation, and definitely no storytelling, did. The understanding was that where politeness trumpeted intimacy, and where rectitude was given its due, people would get along. Best to be nicely bland and blandly nice. Best to wear your linguistic trousers rolled. To stay so buttoned and pursed and everyway tapped down, one had to avoid lively banter at any cost. Otherwise, folks might think you were interesting. They might even think you were interested in them.

Language was a put off, a brush back. Neutral, unadorned speech served to conserve the city's weird self-definition as a community where individuals, if so needy, could always travel to Buffalo for kicks. Uni-sentenced Billy the Garbage Man remained a good neighbour, for sure, and though I was always terrified when my ball landed in the MacGregor yard, obliging a Boo Radley-like foray into a child's haunting, the family was certainly no bother to share a property line with, or a lawn. And yet, had our respective houses bent like bulrushes, they would have touched heads in a storm. Five feet of grass separated their bungalow from our A-frame. My bedrooms, first in the dormer upstairs and then the bunker basement, both had windows that gazed across that chasm, and for years and years I looked out at our phantom neighbours and wondered – this is no exaggeration – what Mrs MacGregor's voice sounded like and if their daughters, including one close to my own age, had by some Old Testament curse been born mute. Even as a boy, this muteness, this grim reserve, made me lonely and sad. It made me wonder early about the curious ways of adults.

For music in 1960s Willowdale we sang 'God Save the Queen' at Blessed Trinity elementary school and 'Kumbayah' at cub camp. If asked for a list of top five songs of my childhood, three of them would be jingles from cartoons or TV commercials. (The other two would be the French lullabies my Franco-Ontarian mother sang to her children.) You'll look better in a sweater washed in Woolite. George, George, George of the Jungle, friend to you and me. Poor little road-runner never bothers anyone. I remember channelling the Elmer Fudd part in the great Bugs Bunny cartoon on route to school some mornings. "Kill the Wabbit," I sang, timidly at first, fearful of squinting windows and grown-up frowns. But then, thrilling to the silliness, I let my voice climb in faux-operatic gravitas and even dared raise an imaginary sword, for smiting: "KILL THE WABBIT!"

Strange as it may sound, those TV jingles and cartoon lines were a thrill to sing and recite. The words had cadence and charge. They acted unafraid of wit or cleverness. My hunger for smart language, for speech as play, began in mid-childhood, and for a long time I could not afford to be fussy. A friend's father hailed from Ireland, and though his accent bent my non-pliant ear, I still drank in his every word, often contenting myself with the beats of his skittery, breakneck speech. My own father, born and raised in the cloistered abbey of the Ottawa-Irish community, had a small repertoire of sayings that I likewise pondered and mouthed and unconsciously praised for their liveliness. "He couldn't fight his way out of a paper bag," he would say. Or else: "That one is dumb as a sack of hammers." There were a few mild expletives, including "Jesus, Mary and Joseph," along with a charming residue of the Ottawa Valley accent he had heard as a boy. For 'potatoes' my father would say "*bha-day-does*," and then would smile in amusement, and slight apology, at this quirk. Unbeknownst to him, or to my mother, whose English held echoes of those French cradle songs, I also declaimed her songs – "*Sur le pont, D'Avignon, on y dance*" – and his few idioms as well on those walks to school. "He's dumb as a sack of hammers!" I would assure any dogs I met on the road to Blessed Trinity School at Finch and Bayview.

Kill the wabbit! the animals could easily have replied.

No doubt, there are good reasons why Canadians still tend to use language and – arguably – write books the ways we do. The lingering effects of linguistic colonialism, especially among the family compact of Lower Canada, is an obvious one. Likewise the palletizing nature of American popular culture, with its one-English-works-for-all-markets rule. The impulse to position ourselves in the mid-Atlantic, as defence against cultural assimilation, may be a factor as well. But as I tried to hint with Roddy Doyle's 'Dunphy and chips' and Réjean Ducharme's 'le cric crock,' other cultures treat their languages as though they inhabit them. They live in language as surely as they live in cities and towns. I wonder, though, how much we live in Canadian English. I wonder if we're still not more tenants, or perhaps weekenders, in this linguistic space, yet awaiting passage on the next boat back to the motherland. I am talking, of course, about the occupation of a territory that is at once within our imaginations and, naturally, where we actually do call home. Only is it a real home if we have only a functional relationship with that most basic component – our speech?

1999

IDIOM-PROOF:

How To Talk Canadian

After an audience screening of the rough-cut of *Shrek*, it was decided that there was a problem with the film's title character, a lonely ogre played by Mike Myers. The problem wasn't the dialogue or the actor. It was the accent. Myers, a native of Toronto, had delivered his lines in his regular voice, making the creature a southern Ontario ogre. That just wasn't funny.

Myers soon recognized this himself. He re-dubbed the part in a Scottish brogue that reminded him of the voices his own mother, who was English, used when she read fairy tales to her children in their home in the Toronto suburb of Scarborough. Crowds roared at the Scottish Shrek and were forgiving of instances where the actor, according to at least one critic, lapsed into Canadian.

Some might take insult at being told their accent isn't worthy of an animated green monster. But Canadians are more likely to be grateful that Mike Myer's linguistic passport was read at all. Canadian speech is so subtle it is routinely mistaken for non-existent, or at least indistinguishable from generic American.

There isn't a uniform Canadian accent, just as there isn't a uniform British, or American, or Indian accent. But there are definite characteristics to Canadian speech, and they show very little variation from the Ottawa River to the Pacific. Generally, speech patterns in Canada weigh anchor in the mid-Atlantic. Our talk is clipped and evenly cadenced. It disavows drawl. Linguists do write about the modest 'Canadian raising' phenomenon. The initial vowel element in certain words is spoken higher in the mouth than in American versions, with the glide to the second element being shorter. We say 'couch' with an 'ouch' and our 'house' rhymes with 'lout,' rather than 'loud.' We are rumoured to say *ah-boot* for 'about,' though that may simply be how others hear these high and fast diphthongs.

Not all experts are convinced that Canadian English is faring well. While the McGill Dialectology and Sociolinguistics laboratory in Montreal is studying regional differences in Canadian speech, academic papers elsewhere chart its steady disappearance, usually through assimilation with American. The more hard-headed even declare the notion of a Canadian dialect a myth, fabricated to bolster a wobbly national identity. According to Henry Rogers, a linguist at the University of Toronto, language in more densely populated areas does show a greater susceptibility to change. We drift towards the pronunciation that surrounds us. Cities – where most Canadians now live – aren't necessarily the places to preserve existing accents, or acquire new ones.

Dialects, of course, are comprised equally of idioms and word choices. The most recent *Collins English Dictionary* includes some 150 new "Canadian" terms. "Status Indian" and "equalization payment" probably won't excite linguistic pride. But a "saw off," for a compromise, and "idiot strings," for the ties that keep children's mittens to their coats, are lively enough. Then there are our drinking words: a "two-four" and a "twenty-sixer" and a "mickey" of rye, often sipped out of a brown paper bag.

That said, Canadian English, at least from Ottawa westwards, can't come close to Irish or Australian in terms of wit and inventiveness. It can't even rival the other Canadian dialect, the one belonging to Newfoundland. Geographical isolation, along with deep Scottish and Irish roots, ensured that East Coast pronunciation would remain distinct from that of the more deracinated middle Canada. Dictionaries exist that catalogue the fragile vocabularies of Prince Edward Island and Nova Scotia's Cape Breton and South Shore, most likely for posterity. But out on the Rock there is less need to be archival. Speech there remains musical and loose and nicely barbed.

An off-the-cuff remark by the Newfoundland actress Mary Walsh, who declared someone to be "still having the mark of the bucket on her arse," started the television critic John Doyle wondering how she gets away with it. Doyle, who recalled the insult from his own Irish childhood, concluded that the line would have been unacceptable on Canadian TV "had it been delivered in less colourful language, and without the accent." On another occasion Walsh slagged the politician Preston Manning. "I've always enjoyed Mr. Manning's speeches," she said of the Alberta populist, "and I'm sure they're even more edifying in the original German." The way Mary Walsh pronounced 'edifying' – *edy-fie-ink*, hammering each syllable – lent the joke a snarl, the disrespect gleeful.

But the real question may be this: Do most Canadians want to leave such a strong impression? The language impulses of the rest of the English-speaking nation have always tended towards moderation, and sometimes disguise. Generations of Canadian actors and newsreaders have counted on both to launch careers in the States.

There could also be a class dimension to how the majority of us talk. Middle-class societies tend to avoid strong or idiosyncratic speech, finding such verbal energy unruly. For all their appeal, regional idioms, especially those from the historically poorer regions of Canada, with their culturally-engrained admiration of word-play and irreverence, have made scant impact on the wider nation. We haven't taken into our collective mouths "having a scoff" for a meal or being "stogged up" for stuffed, or of declaring about black flies: "If you kill one, fifty more come to its funeral," as they do in Nova Scotia's South Shore. We don't delight in repeating that "scluttery" means fatty or that a guy who has "chowdered" something has messed it up.

If we had, perhaps Mike Myers might have hung tough with his Canadian accent. Shrek, after all, would have made a fine Newfoundland ogre.

2003

ELOQUENCE LOST:

The Death Of The Topographical Mind

At age sixteen I discovered how old books talk. In my local mall was a Coles outlet selling classic novels for a dollar each. The print was squinting and the bindings were of cardboard. The novels seemed chosen mostly for their brevity, and maybe with an eye to readers who liked their tales tall and ripping. For a year or so I read only about Swift's Gulliver and Defoe's Robinson Crusoe, the Kipling of *Captains Courageous* and *Kidnapped* by Robert Louis Stevenson.

They were wondrous and thrilling, these eighteenth- and nineteenth-century worlds of adventure, and never more so than when characters opened their mouths. Everyone spoke with such refinement and, often enough, at such length. Even the most rough-hewn sorts, their dialogue littered with "arrghs" and "ayes" and other piratical grunts, possessed a verbal quality I had not encountered in my own life.

That quality was eloquence, and I was, in fact, already too late to hear much of it out of the mouths of the living. Eloquence once referred to formal discourse. Of late the term has come to be more generally defined as fluent and graceful talk, particularly the kind that persuades. Grounded in spoken language that derived its cadence and grammar from the written word, eloquence was equally rooted in a widespread admiration for, and emulation of, oratory. By the mid-1970s, when I was first taking an interest in such speech, both those traditions were on the wane.

Now they are nearly disappeared, and how we talk is much changed for it. Valley Girl speak, popularized by the eponymous 1982 Frank Zappa song, is enshrined as North American lingo. Young people, with their penchant for slang and verbal disfluencies – those pauses we, like, insert into our speech while seeking the, um, right term – are often tagged as the worst language offenders. But it is increasingly acceptable for adults to aspire to no greater linguistic heights. Forty-year-old men refer to each other as "dude" and grown women can deliver a "what-ever" the snap of any character in the teen film *Clueless*.

Whether or not the fate of eloquence is cause for lament may depend on what kind of language you favour. That, in turn, could reflect how your mind has been conditioned, both to listen and to speak.

Nearly two decades ago Neil Postman tracked the demise of the "typographical mind." His seminal *Amusing Ourselves to Death: Public Discourse in the Age of Show Business* used the 1858 debates between Abraham Lincoln and Stephen Douglas as an instance of a vanished culture. Audiences of ordinary citizens, including one crowd estimated at 15,000, sat on benches for hours listening to Lincoln and Douglas debate slavery and abolition. They were able to do so, Postman explained, because their intellects had been conditioned by the rigors of written language. They had the training and the patience, as well as the appetite. "Language as pure print," he called it.

But the "age of typography" has long been supplanted by the "age of television." Starting in the 1950s, public business, be it politics, religion or even education, had to be recast to work on TV, a medium that promotes, in his view, "incoherence and triviality." Intellects shifted as well, along with conventions of speech. This is language as pure pixels, in effect.

Hence the sound bite and the sentence fragment and the shyness about sounding too high-and-mighty before the camera. The linguist John McWhorter, taking up Postman's argument, believes eloquence was doomed the moment public figures abandoned "speech" in favor of "talk." McWhorter writes in *Doing Our Own Thing: The Degradation of Language and Music and Why We Should, Like, Care* that, once, "talking was for conversation. In public or on paper, one used a different kind of language, just as we use forks and knives instead of eating with our hands." Now everyone, including politicians, seems content to eat with their hands, everywhere and all the time.

Our low regard for rhetoric may make traditional eloquence impossible. "Mere rhetoric" is the favoured put down, implying that any verbal conceit or flourish cloaks a lack of substance and/or sincerity. Politicians strike folksy notes as a result, preferring to err on the side of the faux-humble.

The contemporary mellifluousness of Bill Clinton, for instance, engendered as much suspicion among Americans as it did praise. Similarly, George W. Bush's admirers apparently find his limited verbal facility a sign of trustworthiness. Ask most people for a list of great orators, and they inevitably draw from either the language-as-print era, or the infancy of language-as-pixels: Roosevelt and Churchill, John Kennedy and Martin Luther King. It may be that we get the public orators our private speech deserves.

Closer to home, Rex Murphy has chided Canadian politicians for their dull, formulaic language. "It's a strange rhetorical competition that is ashamed of rhetoric," the broadcaster and columnist wrote of a televised election debate, "a strange public-speaking contest that is embarrassed by eloquence." But then Murphy, an uncommonly eloquent man with a penchant for periodic sentences and ten-buck words, is himself an anomaly.

John McWhorter suspects Americans have become too colloquial to ever be eloquent again. The suspicion can surely be extended to their northern neighbours. Our cultures "thrill most to English yoked to orally based charisma," be it rap music, spoken word poetry, or literary authors with chatty styles. A flare for the verbally transgressive is equalled by a growing indifference to, and discomfort with, the "stringent artifice of written language."

At the same time, we are also now in the thrall of new technologies at least the match of television's impact in the 1960s and 70s. Critics fear cellphones and text messaging are further dumbing down conversations. Language, then, as pure digital? "Every change in our principal means of communication changes how we communicate," notes the scholar Derek de Kerckhove. Youth culture is certainly being influenced by digital language, a lingo notable for its spotty grammar and preference for codes and signs over the alphabet. Should hypertext ever migrate into the mouths of its adherents, it will produce some curious slang indeed.

Like it or not, that slang will probably be appropriate for our informal, impatient, post-literate age. The language will suit the way we live, and the ways we talk – or don't talk, perhaps – about our lives.

As Steven Pinker has noted, every generation tends to believe that language is in decline. John McWhorter, at least, is careful to point out that we actually know little about how regular folk spoke in the pre-microphone past. Listening to, say, a New York cabdriver in the 1940s, as cited in *Doing Our Own Thing*, suggests that too much nostalgia for a supposedly more refined era would be a mistake. "Youse fellas," the cabbie is captured saying, "ya always got da same habit."

It is true, however, that the cabdriver a half-century ago still wanted his elected representatives to express themselves using elevated language and high rhetoric. For a variety of reasons, we no longer expect or even wish politicians to perform that function. Nor do many of us look any longer to pulpits for inspiration of any kind.

Maybe there is a link between speech and subject. Could eloquence come more easily when topics involve honour and valour, faith and responsibility? You don't hear those matters discussed much anymore, in either public or private life. But then I am speaking as an example of a cross between a pure-print and pure-pixels mind, conditioned as much by the old books I read as by the television I grew up watching.

2004

CAN'T THINK FOR THE RACKET:

Music And Prose

The shape of the sentence, the song of its syllables, the rhythm of its movement, is the movement of the imagination, too; it is the allocation of the things of the world to their place in the world of the word; it is the configuration of its concepts – not to neglect them – like the stars, which are alleged to determine the fate of we poor creatures who bear their names, suffer their severities, enjoy their presence of mind and the sigh of their light in our night . . . all right . . . all right . . . okay; the glow of their light in our darkness.

—FROM "THE MUSIC OF PROSE" BY WILLIAM GASS

I

Graham played in a band in Tillsonburg. I had taken guitar lessons for a couple of years at a studio off Yonge Street. We were both seventeen, Junior Rangers stationed in the bush near Timmins. He was small town cool, small town cornered. I hailed from the suburbs but was, I already sensed, bound elsewhere. We alone had packed guitars with our gear that summer-that-Elvis-died. A broken sauna by the dock became the lone site in camp to practise without having to suffer requests for 'Stairway To Heaven.' Though Graham handled the rhythm parts back home, he was desperate to take a few leads. Except the lead guitarist, a prick, won't give over even one solo. I had yawned and bluffed my way through Segovia exercises and 'Classical Gas' in Toronto, my teacher, a draft dodger with a ponytail and an appetite for weed – his plaid shirts reeked of it, the smell, I decided, of rock and roll – cursing his bad luck in students. I had no music, basically. None in my parents' house and very little in my head.

Did I want to jam some twelve-bar blues? Graham asked. Support him on my acoustic while he learned how to lead? Please and thank you, I answered.

He pinched beer bottle necks between his fingers. He dragged on a cigarette while plucking notes, or else tucked the filters into the machine head, a la Keith Richards. Graham had played ZZ Top for hours in his mind while picking tobacco leaves on farms around Southern Ontario. School was already done for him. A drop out, Grade Ten. That left tobacco work, seasonal stuff with the ministry, and the band. Unbelievable, playing in a band. Covers of the Stones and Zeppelin, Lynyrd Skynyrd and the Allman Brothers; gigs, some bad but some oh so good, the bars crowded and sweaty and everyone getting fucked up. As for the girls . . . well, Graham got some. Did he ever. But better still than the girls were the feelings that rocked (not rolled) him when he played. He tried to explain. It felt . . . you know . . . it felt . . . like that, you know? Then he'd smile in apology, his brown eyes sleepy. He, too, wore plaid shirts and a leather vest, like my guitar teacher. His bushy sideburns were Neil Young.

(Actually, I didn't know how "it" felt. Not at all. But I just smiled back, happy to hear him talk.)

One week into our after-work-hours jam, I was still bad. I strummed chunky chords, missed beats or landed them flat, scrambled from E to A or E to B#7 too early or too late, or else on time but without snap. Graham grinned at my ineptness and kept on picking out runs, nodding to himself when he traced a nifty line. Two weeks into it, I had the sequence down – four/two/two/two/one/one – and the grind: thump-de-thump, thump-de-thump . . . S L I D E . . . thump-de-thump, thump-de-thump. I had the basics, minus any flourishes, but I still didn't have, according to Graham, the thing. The thing? I had to ask. Three parts to it, he replied. The groin thing. The space thing. The think thing.

The groin came first. Play less, he advised me, but make love to each and every chord you sound. Make love? I said. Screw, he clarified. Screw? I echoed. It's about humping, Graham said plainly. Humping a girl. HUMP-de-HUMP, he demonstrated, closing his eyes while he pounded the strings. HUMP-de-HUMP-de HUMP.

Got it, I said.

You're not? . . . Graham said one day.

Not what?

Tell me you're not.

I'm not a virgin, I said. No way.

Next came the space thing. I was having trouble with the shapes of the tunes. After five minutes, I would look to him for a sign that the number was winding down. Five minutes later again, I'd plead cramped fingers or the need for a slash. Every time we stopped, no matter how long we'd been going, Graham would frown in disappointment. No end to twelve-bar blues, his frown inferred. It's not that kind of space. What kind of space was twelve-bar? Once you were inside it, he tried to say (I am helping him with words here, as he helped me with music), it was vast as a summer sky and fathomless as the bush and even though – for sure, even though – you were playing the same chords in the same sequence again and again, each round was unique, producing a singular groove, a solitary spark, because the space you were in when you jammed the blues had neither any ending up ahead nor any start-up back behind. It had only the middle, the pure bullshit-free sweet moment, and weren't you lucky to be there.

What was the sweet moment? That was the think thing. In twelve-bar, Graham said, no thinking was allowed. Whatever you do, don't think. Whatever you decide to play, don't ponder why you did it. For sure, whatever you are feeling – ah, feelings, again – don't fuss or fret or worry about figuring it out. Don't figure anything out. Just play.

II

Four years later, in a pub in Adare, County Limerick, Ireland, I pulled pints and halves of lager and poured drams and small ones and even fixed the occasional pot of tea for ten hours a day, six days a week. Customers were mostly local, men in caps and wellies and tweed jackets, their dogs on the sidewalk outside. The Limerick accent was susurration, Cork patter meshed with Kerry drawl. The pub was in a hotel, meaning I spent off-hours in a grim staff room listening to round-the-table conversations among waiters and kitchen crew.

Come here a minute, you, one would begin.

He's gas.

A gas man.

Gas ticket, wha.

And yourself?

Get away.

That's gas.

Don't you know.

Come here a minute.

Or else, during quiet evenings tending bar with my profane boss:

A right wanker, that one, he would say.

Who?

The eejit by the window.

The right wanker?

That's him.

The eejit?

Miserable cunt, is what he is.

Also a fucker? I would ask.

And a piss-artist. An omadoon.

Ah.

You know the one.

I do.

You have to.

Of course.

You haven't a clue who I'm talking about, have you?

Not really.

Fucking Yanks.

Canadian, actually.

I would drum my fingertips on the counter to the cadences of his speech: the steady measures and glottal stops, the snare drum syncopation. Meal times in the staff room, a half-dozen employees trashing each other with dexterity and glee – 'taking the piss,' they called it, or 'codding' or 'giving a bit of the stick' – my foot would likewise tap to the beat. Language as cadence, as vocables, as scat. Language as music. Slowly, though, I began to desire to hear meanings of a more conventional sort. I began to want the words – spoken, after all, in what was technically also my mother tongue – if not yet to lie down on the page and be prose, then to at least register as thought and feeling, while still retaining their beat. Not that I dared bring a pen and notebook into the room that summer in Adare. Not that I dared do much more than grin myself silly listening and tap my fingers on the tabletop, until someone would invariably say:

Would you ever quit the taping.

Sorry.

It's murder on the skull.

Sorry.

Fucking Yanks.

Canadian, actually.

Two years later again, I did a Master's degree in Anglo-Irish literature in Dublin. At first, it seemed perfect. In Yeats and Joyce, Beckett and Synge, Flann O'Brien and Patrick Kavanagh, I found all that staff hall banter, all that crack, translated onto the page, discursive and argumentative and perfect of pitch. Yet the pages, the books, sounded oddly muffled and fuzzy, and it took a while to figure out why. I had forgotten the music I first heard in Limerick. I was still too hard of hearing to read Irish literature.

Finding a classmate to read the texts aloud with might have done it. Too shy to ask, I turned instead to the city for help. Hawkers in Pearse Street and tinkers on the O'Connell Street Bridge. Old ladies in Herbert Park and rugby players at Belfield. Ironically, what they said mattered less now than *how* they played it. I memorized phrases by their cadences, repeating them over and over to myself until I registered their musical 'sense' and could, in effect, tap-tap my fingers to them as well. A hawker's cry of "Lighters, five for a pound" became *Lada, lie-di-di-di-di*; a scolding 'Your man's a right gobshite' ended up *Dadah, de-dah-de-dah-de-dah*. Don't talk, I told myself as I wandered Dublin – just listen. Don't think – just play. Then I would return to James Joyce or Samuel Beckett, a passage from J.M. Synge's *The Playboy of the Western World* or Flann O'Brien's *The Third Policeman*, and I would hear the literary language for what it surely was: dark and funny, excoriating and raw.

"My mother was the first to go," O'Brien's narrator declares, "and I can remember a fat man with a red face and black suit telling my father that there was no doubt where she was, that he could be as sure of that as he could of anything else in this vale of tears. But he did not mention where and as I thought the whole thing was very private and that might be back on Wednesday, I did not ask him."

In Dublin I wrote some of my first stories. Mostly, though, I took dictation. Ear to head to pen: vocal exercises – do-re-mi-fa-so-la-ti-do – before the actual recital began, the real words emerged.

III

A friend, a Belfast inner-émigré named Seamus, helped run a Friday night dance at a G.A.A. (Gaelic Athletic Association) club in a tough Southside neighbourhood. It was 1984, and certain Dublin youths were smoking fags and guzzling cans of Harp, collecting the dole and not giving a fuck about much. Jeans jackets and shaved heads were the uniform; uncut heroin and skinhead rage were the concerns. Seamus asked me along to work the door with him. There had been trouble previous Friday nights between rival crowds, *go feck yourselves* and gobs of spit and even a few wild swings, and he wanted another body to brace the event's foundation. Also, he thought we'd make an effective team. His accent – Belfast by birth, hard man or even IRA-on-the-lamb by wild speculation – might make the lads pause and wonder if he had his own rage-switch, along with a taste for knee-capping. My accent – Toronto by birth, American TV by implication – might make those same lads grin and laugh and leave it alone.

The hall filled quickly to beyond fire regulations. The door Seamus and I were watching was soon barred: exit only out the back, and no re-admittance. Two hundred boyos, along with their birds, pogoed and body-slammed on the dance floor. Sweat mingled with damp fabric and the cigarette smoke being fumigated from clothing and hair by the commotion. With its dropped ceiling and cinderblock walls, the room had the acoustics of a clapped-out stereo speaker. Bass notes, busted-woofer-wonky, entered the soles of boots and climbed the legs to the groin, causing various small quakes, and then climbed further to the chest, where they induced palpitations, before fading at the neck, the head largely unscrambled.

U2, North-side Dubliners with God and attitude and regrettable mullet-hair cuts, were just that winter signing up their generation with

'Sunday Bloody Sunday' and 'New Years Day.' But it was their infancy hit of 1981, "I Will Follow," that convinced the G.A.A. club crowd to enlist. The tune's firecracker drum beat and wide, floating guitar riffs seemed to tilt the floor. The thrust was fierce, like a boat that lists, sending cargo and passengers skittering to a gunwale. Then the boat rights itself; then it lists again in the opposite direction. Bono sang "If you walk away, walk away, I will follow," and so did every kid in the club, arms raised and fists pumping: "If you walk away, walk away, I will follow."

Their song, I recognized at once. Their culture.

Next, the DJ spun Thin Lizzy's cover of the pub standard 'Whiskey in the Jar.' I had always assumed the version to be a lark. The band were rockers, all power chords and strutting poses ('The Boys are Back in Town' was a huge hit), and were fronted by a black Dubliner named Phil Lynott. Lynott wasn't black, as in protestant, but black, as in skin colour – a peppercorn in a bowl of homogenous Irish milk. But, to my astonishment, the tune was greeted with such a roar it could have been mistaken for the cries of a ship's crew as the vessel threatened to capsize yet again. Lynott sang: "Whack fol the dahdeoho" and so did nearly everyone in the hall: "Whack fol the dahdeoho." Then the chorus, proclaimed with the same joyful possessiveness as U2. "There's whiskey in the jar!"

Their song as well. Their culture.

A few months later I was renting an old schoolhouse in west Galway. A schoolhouse in a bog; a bog at the foot of the Twelve Bens, moon mountains covered in spongy heather and drooping fuchsia. Desolation was my preferred landscape and solitude my artiste lifestyle. One morning I awoke to the murmur of cows in the yard, and went out for a chat. One evening I rescued a German who'd been waiting in the rain since early afternoon for a lift, and cooked him dinner. Slugs the size of sausages plummeted from my ceiling. Curtains billowed behind supposedly sealed windows. I had no phone, and didn't want one. The postman delivered mail on a bicycle, when there was any.

The house came with a radio. English RTE (Radio Television Eireann) provided news; Irish RTE played music. I was writing a novel to Irish RTE, a book named after a lament composed two centuries

earlier by a blind harpist named O'Carolan. 'Blind Mary' was the
name of the tune, and the manuscript. The story took place in present
day County Limerick. Irish characters were wankers and omadoons
who thrashed to U2 and Thin Lizzy. The Canadian character, a bar-
tender in a hotel, was American TV, more or less. I wrote by a kitchen
window that opened onto the road and the bog. More weather rolled
past than cars. A formation an hour, I reckoned; a day of sunshine or
rain, or of clouds riven with light, back in Canada might last twenty
minutes in Connemara, before being supplanted. Socked-in skies still
vaulted, though, and clear skies climbed so high they wound up mir-
roring themselves against a filament that I imagined, only half-
fancifully, to be the curve of the earth's ozone. Nights were as deep as
certain wells. Stars rarely shone through the strata of cloud.

One afternoon I put down my pen at the opening notes of a reel
played on solo flute. The musician had the breathy style I associated
with prog-rocker Jethro Tull. From the start, the music was fluid. I
turned up the volume and watched through the window as a weather
formation, stately as a regatta, floated out into the Atlantic ocean to the
melody, wisps of angel's breath scurrying along the margin between
earth and sky. A second reel emerged from the first. Now the flutist was
adding ornamentation – triplets and trills and grace notes. Certain
notes were stretched and held. Others were blunted or bitten. All manner of non-thoughts flashed through my mind while I listened and
watched. Everything seemed in motion, in flight; everything seemed at
once exact and permanent, fleeting and evanescent. Like the weather.
Like a young Canadian in a school house in Galway.

"Matt Molloy," the announcer said, naming the great musician,
lately a member of The Chieftains. Then, as if he knew I was listening,
the voice added in English: "The Irish soul."

I sat at the kitchen table for a long while after that, staring at my
manuscript. It wasn't that I couldn't move; rather, I wasn't quite back
in my body, wasn't quite returned from where the music had taken me.
I looked down at the pages and up at the sky, then down at the pages
again, and decided that the book I was working on could only be bad.
Not phoney or fake: just tone deaf and, perhaps, touristy. Because this
wasn't mine, this place and its music; these weren't mine, these voices
and their meanings. Could I ever make any of it mine, or at least

borrow? Landscape in a novel, I already understood, was never an actual subject. Always, settings are a portal onto a writer's real concerns. Maybe. But not back then, when I was just twenty-four.

IV

I never published the novel named after the lament by the 18th-century harpist. But in 1994 I did publish a novel about a feckless Canadian who travels to Ireland to better understand his Irish father, a fiddler who died before he was born. It involves much weather and landscape and traditional music, and has characters who might be wankers and do like early U2. In 1996 I also published a novel about a feckless Canadian who travels to China in part to escape his mother and better understand his father, who he, too, never knew. Self-knowledge is on his mind as well. I titled that book after a piece of Chinese music I first heard in a Beijing concert hall. One listen to the concerto 'Butterfly Lovers' and I was lost again. Lost in the music. Lost – even more improbably than in Ireland – in the landscape, the culture, that had produced such an expression of soul. I have always been a sucker for a good tune well told. I can't ever seem to think clearly for the racket.

V

Nothing Canadian so far, I realize. Nothing about a childhood in suburban Toronto and a logging town in Northern Ontario. Growing up in Willowdale, there was Gordon Lightfoot and the Clancy Brothers on the radio and 'The Best Of' Ginette Reno and Barbara Streisand on the helmet-shaped Eight-Track player in the dining room. There were also my father's cassettes of Hank Williams and Johnny Cash. That was about it for music in our Willowdale house, unless you counted the French nursery rhymes my mother sang to her children – *Sur le pont d'Avignon, on est dance, on est dance* and *La grenouille dans les temps – sauté, sauté, tout le temps!* – or acknowledged the mouth music of her franglais, practised during summers in Blind River, and otherwise on the phone with one of her twelve sisters. Conversations between the

Fallu siblings shared languages the way a ventriloquist shared voices. Exchanges that I first heard as *"bloobybloobyblooby* . . . Well, if that's what she wants, eh? . . . *bloobybloobyblooby* . . . . You just never know with those people, do you . . ." I later came to appreciate sounded like this: "*Bien oui, bien oui, c'est triste, tellement triste* . . . Yes, we'll be up there the third week of July, once Dave starts his holidays . . . *Non, pas problem – Il ne comprehend pas, pas encore.*"

Nothing in my Canadian house, unless I try to account for that music and culture, which, truth be told, I have scarcely begun to do. Or unless I register the fact that the first time I was ever so taken with a remark about literature that I taped it to the wall of my bedroom at university, it was a comment by a Canadian, and concerned the relationship between music and prose. "If the music of a sentence is right," the critic Northrop Frye wrote, "the sense will take care of itself." Northrop Frye said that about language? I could hardly believe it myself. But I have loved the sentence, and the sentiment, ever since, without patriotic intent or – come to think of it – enough reflection.

If the music of a sentence
is right
The sense will take care
of itself.

1998

BOOKS

BUTTERFLY INTO MAN:

A Parable About Stories

The written word is weak. Many people prefer life to it. Life gets your blood going, and it smells good.

—ANNIE DILLARD

People say it all the time. That would make a good novel, they say. You should write it down. Usually, they are referring to a story fragment or even an anecdote, and mean that something borrowed from real life seems to possess the coherence and tidiness of fiction. If a tale is messy and vague and meanders like a toddler's monologue, it must be authentic. If it is crafted and rounded, gathering momentum and out-lining arc, it must be made-up. There is only one explanation for stories that aren't narrative muddle and thematic disaster – they belong in books.

It's a nice, if backhanded compliment to the novel form. These days, it is also a sly threat: be useful, novel, or else. Tell me a tale that makes sense and so will, in effect, have an obvious utility, if only as diversion and entertainment. Beginning, middle and end. Direction and purpose. Even a moral, a lesson. Tell it, in effect, like it isn't. Keep it not-so-real. The fury aimed at books that deny readers these unities is, from a certain regard, understandable. No page-turning plot or cin-ema-familiar characters? No ending-that-ties all strands into pretty bows? I can go drink with my buddies if I want incoherence. I can try discussing feelings with my husband if I desire a muddle.

There is no telling some people that novels are imaginative spaces and states of mindfulness. Simulacrums of being, waking and other-wise. Enchantments, drawn from the well of archetypes we all embody and all need to drink from daily, nightly, to help us live – even if we don't know that we know any of this. No telling them that fictions are assemblies of words reeling over the landscapes of their narratives, happy to do the job of communicating intent but equally inclined to etch loops and parabolas in the sky, just for the hell of it. Aesthetic rebels, those literary birds.

For sure, there is no telling some readers that a 'great story' does not a great book make. That great stories are to great books what clothes are to the man: nice, but not essential. *Heart of Darkness* is a ripper and *Pride and Prejudice* a girl-meets-a-boy-at-a-dance. But *To the Lighthouse*, about a woman pondering the day ahead (an ordinary one), or *Tristram Shandy*, concerning a character trying just to be born? (He doesn't manage it.) To each novel according to its aptitudes and needs.

Ever since I can remember, tales that question the divide between dreaming and wakefulness have spoken to me in the manner that God apparently talks to others. As a child I substituted myself for the characters in books I was reading, the better to enter that dream and exit, perhaps, that wakefulness. As a teenager I heard in Prospero's ode to mortality a joyful assertion of the immortality found in repetition. Of course our lives are rounded with a sleep. How else can they be such stuff as dreams are made on? Even Samuel Beckett's *Waiting for Godot*, a play rarely accused of being life-affirmative, left a warm feeling in at least one Toronto high-school student. Naturally Vladimir and Estrogen wait for Godot to not appear. How else can they be sure they are still inside the stuff of life – i.e. the stuff of dreams? Vladimir says as much in Act II, does he not? "Was I sleeping, while the others suffered?" he wonders. "Am I sleeping now?"

Well, kind of.

Had I been asked to defend this cheerful take on Beckett, and then been seized by a premonitory self-awareness about an impulse that remained un-self-examined for decades, I would have replied as follows: *Waiting for Godot*, being an imagined space, a book of reeling words, isn't supposed to be life-affirmative. It is supposed to be geography-affirmative. The geography of where? The place where day and night and light and dark, sleep and wake and dream and undream, meet and then dissolve.

Or butterfly and man? I first read Lao Zhi's parable when I was maybe sixteen, I did not know Taoism from Maoism then, or the One Thing (the Tao) from Wild Thing (die dong) But a single exposure to the parable, or, rather, a single afternoon spent pondering a few lines of cryptic oriental wisdom while lying in grass gazing up at etchings of bird flight and processions of clouds, and it was forever lodged equally in my consciousness, like Bible stories learned at mass, and my subconscious, like the moral codes acquired by breathing-in, breathing-out, a Catholic childhood.

The venerable Lao Zhi falls asleep by a stream and dreams he is a butterfly, flying about and feeling good in his being. He awakens and is himself again, the venerable Lao Zhi. Or is he? Formerly, he had been a man dreaming he was a butterfly. Might he not now be a butterfly dreaming he is a man?

Granted, I was a drifting kid, and then a floating teen, and then a young man so trapped in the cold snows of a dream, to paraphrase W.B. Yeats, that I had to regularly wipe my brow clear. At university I had a friend who was studying philosophy. He did most of his reading in the front room of the college library. I would visit him there, or glance in the window and watch him read, hour after hour, day after day, in between my wanderings around campus and downtown. Much as I often wished to, I could not join my friend at his desk for very long and likewise open a book – Sterne, say, or Virginia Woolf, instead of Plato or Kant – and just, well, read it. I had to walk instead.

It wasn't only restlessness and jittery nerves that kept me on my feet. It was an uncertainty about whether I was a student dreaming of being a butterfly or a butterfly dreaming of being a student. Instinctively, I saw most things as unstable, including my own self. Intuitively, I took reality to be fleeting and floating, impermanent permanence, like those cloud regattas and bird sketches. Lines from a Theodore Roethke poem I had learned in Grade Thirteen captured the feeling: "What falls away is always. And is near," Roethke wrote.

I was mostly thinking about books back then. Now I am mostly writing them. A middle-aged reverie-artist, still restless and jittery and uncertain about the reality of those divides, I remain a devotee of the butterfly parable. The devotion is now professional, a working, rather than walking, preoccupation. The condition the parable outlines, and implicitly celebrates, is the one, I more and more think, aspired to by serious works of art. Or rather, it is the condition experienced by the reader when in the company of a great novel.

The books themselves needn't be drifting or floating. Quite the opposite. The majority of novels remain solidly about solid stuff: the ways and means of societies, the patterns of human affairs, a reflection, in turn, of the patterning of the human mind. Rather, it is their power to release us from our one reality, and our one self, and dissolve us into all those other realities and selves that induces such an effect. How small and tawdry we are, after all. How vast and magnificent are we all, when cast as butterfly into man and woman into butterfly. Neither am I a reader dreaming of being a character nor a character dreaming of reading a book. Madame Bovary, c'est nous.

That power, by the way, isn't easily summoned in fictions of conventional opinion and received technique. A culture that discourages its artists from creating bold simulacrums and wild enchantments is one opting for dull, stable sleeps and rote, untransformed wakefulness. How else to experience the wonderment, the awe, if not through assertions that we are such stuff as dreams are made on? How else to feel it, to be delighted, be consoled, be, why not, the One Thing? "I wake to sleep, and take my waking slow," Roethke proclaimed in the same poem. "I learn by going where I have to go."

2006

THE LIFE QUIXOTIC:

Cervantes And The Invention Of Fiction

How about this for inspired literary mischief. A writer is late delivering a promised sequel to his bestselling novel. Ten years late, to be exact, a lifetime in the publishing business. In the interim a rival hiding behind a pseudonym has issued a spurious version that discredits the original. The existence of the counterfeit encourages the writer to hurry quill back to paper. He brings out his Part II, resuming the action a month after Part I ended. His heroes, a knight errant and his faithful squire, are now recognized wherever they go, thanks to that decade-old book, which everyone seems to have read. Knowing they are already the stars of one fiction encourages the pair to embark on further adventures, to provide fresh material for their chronicler. "Does the author promise a second part?" the knight asks a character who has read Part I. He does, the fellow answers, although "he hasn't found it."

The same character summarizes the conventional wisdom about sequels. "Second parts were never very good," he remarks, sounding like a critic of Hollywood blockbusters. So far, this seems a decent play on the fiction of any fiction. But the writer is just warming up. Instead of ignoring his rival's 'fake' sequel, he introduces it in his own 'real' one as "the false, the fictitious, the apocryphal" version of events. Then he reports rumours that the knight and squire from the ersatz book are now loose inside his story as well, pretending to be them. This last twist proves too much for his identity-challenged hero. The poor knight demands that a character who has met the impostors swear before a judge that he – and not the other guy – is authentic. "Because there is no other I in the world," he says.

Sadly for him, that isn't quite true either. For Don Quixote de la Mancha, as the knight is known, is also a fabrication. His real name is Alonso Quixano and he is a middle-aged country squire who has suffered a nervous breakdown. In his delirium – the result, unsurprisingly, of an addiction to chivalric romance novels – he has given himself a grand title and quest, involving slaying giants and sacking castles in the service of Dulcinea del Toboso, his lady-most-fair. She, it so happens, is still another invention, the reality being a buxomy wench called Aldonza Lorenzo that Quixano is too shy to approach.

"The author of our history must be some wise enchanter," Don Quixote says of his creator. As usual, he doesn't know the half of it. Don Quixote doesn't know that *The Ingenious Gentleman Don Quixote de la Mancha* is so in the thrall of its own enchantments that it has been wagging its narrative tail for better than nine hundred pages. He doesn't know that the author, Miguel de Cervantes, while certainly wise, may be adding to the page count in part because he still isn't sure how to close the book he has so brilliantly opened.

When the end finally comes for the knight, it is abrupt. He is made to renounce his delusion and then swiftly expire. He is accorded a nice epitaph – "For it was his great fortune/to live a madman, and die sane" – but is also treated to a proverbial stake-through-the-vampire's-heart, in the form of a document attesting that the corpse is indeed the real Don Quixote. There will be no sequel to the sequel, by the sage enchanter or anyone else.

Miguel de Cervantes published the second part of *Don Quixote* in 1615, a decade after the first volume had granted the sixty-eight-year-old Spaniard unexpected late-career success and a year after the appearance of the spurious Part II. A failed playwright, he appears to have dashed off both parts of his masterpiece, in a hurry less to counter his imitators than return to what he believed was his serious work. In his haste Cervantes allowed his imagination to wander so far and wide from existing prose genres – the pastoral tale and chivalric romance being the most popular at the time – that he ended up in an entirely new form. Today we call that form the modern novel, and credit him with its invention. The author himself died in 1616, his hopes for immortality pinned to a pastoral adventure titled *The Exploits of Persiles and Sigismunda*. It is said to deserve its obscurity.

2005 marks the four-hundredth anniversary of the first instalment of *Don Quixote*. The occasion is being celebrated, predictably enough, with a slew of new books, including a fresh translation by the esteemed Edith Grossman and a re-telling of the tale for children by Barbara Nichol. *The Enamoured Knight*, by novelist Douglas Glover, is an appreciation of the novel. Grossman's translation comes jacketed in an A-list of blurbs, with Carlos Fuentes calling *Don Quixote* "the most eternal novel ever written" and Thomas Mann exclaiming how "its creative genius, critical, free, and human, soars above its age!" Critic Harold Bloom provides an introduction in which he remarks that "this great book contains within itself all the novels that have followed in its wake."

That might be the case. But it might also be true that four centuries after the birth of the novel – a spectacular birth it was, too, like delivering an eighty kilogram baby with a wicked sense of humour and a Mensa IQ – the majority of us hardly recognize the form innovated by Cervantes in the fictions we currently admire. The anniversary offers a chance to revisit the enchantments of *Don Quixote* and also wonder about the state of enchantment in the literature of our own age.

The book tells the most enduring of stories. The journey of the Knight of the Sorrowful Countenance and his squire Sancho Panza in quest of a new self is the search of all humans for fulfillment and meaning. Quixote's insanity is triggered by desire and Duclinea is a figment of his emotional yearning. "Come Sancho," the knight says during a moment of lucidity, "it is enough for me to think and believe that my good Aldonza Lorenzo is beautiful and virtuous . . . I depict her in my imagination as I wish her to be." His search is notable for the questions it asks, not any answers it provides. How do our minds function? How 'real' is reality and how 'unreal' is illusion? And what of our identities: are they fixed and defined or fluid and evolving?

Don Quixote is structurally audacious. Cervantes can't stop messing with the form even while he is still working out the rules for it. He is like the architect who repeatedly complicates his design long after the ground has been broken. By introducing the existence of Part I and the false sequel into Part II, for instance, the author redraws his book, adding further layers of self-awareness and uncertainty. He does so with confidence less in his talent than the expansiveness of the literary genre coming into existence before his eyes. Between those calfskin covers is so much imaginative and aesthetic space. On those blank pages is such freedom.

On those pages as well is going to be plenty of language, doing what language does: constructing and directing its own metaphors and meanings. Cervantes' instinctive receptivity to how language functions has endeared him to an intellectual tradition dating backwards from Foucault to Borges to Nietzsche. In *The Enamoured Knight* Douglas Glover, a smart and enthusiastic student of the multiplicities of *Don Quixote*, is keen to talk literary theory. "At this point," he writes of the intersections at the start of Part II, "*Don Quixote* severs its last tie with verisimilitude, wrenching itself out of the discourse of reality into the relativity of discourses, of languages, as it were, in that floating, postmodern, post-structuralist sense of language as a self-referential system of signs."

Is there anything the novel form designed by Cervantes can't do? The diligent reader of *Don Quixote* may end up answering with a flat no. And yet the author is determined to emphasize one restriction, although he probably thinks of it more as an ironic truth. The novel can't 'do' reality. It can't ever not be a book. Whether we choose to admit it or not, the moment we open a work of fiction we have exited life and entered art. We're down a road and off on a quest, and neither the destination, nor necessarily the purposes, are at first obvious.

Miguel de Cervantes was born in 1547 to an old but impoverished family and wounded in 1571 at the Battle of Lepanto. He was later kidnapped by pirates and sold into slavery in North Africa for five years. Unable to earn a living with his pen, he worked as a tax collector, a job that had him roaming the countryside annoying most everyone he met. He may have begun *Don Quixote* while languishing in prison. Cervantes never earned a peso from the first part of the book, thanks to an unscrupulous publisher, and to his death he remained a marginal figure in Spanish literary circles, the object of derision among more elite wordsmiths.

. *Don Quixote* is an easy psychological match with that biography. Cervantes, either at wit's end with convention or else in a freefall of innovation (or both), builds his knight out of the muddy clay of his own experiences and disappointments. The result is a vividly contemporary psyche. The disillusionment occasioned by repeated failure, the desperation of the poor, even the appeal of madness when reality becomes untenable: the knight and his squire are familiar travellers. That our own era mostly knows Quixote through a sentimental pop-culture digest of the story, where the knight tilts at windmills and dreams the impossible dream, doesn't negate the fact that we can 're-late' to a 400-year-old character. We'll even sing along with the Man of La Mancha, or at least hum the show tunes.

Joining the knight and his guide in their Broadway musical adventure may be the only journey most readers will be able to manage. The novel is long and digressive. The writing is ornate and tirelessly playful. But the more serious 'problem' with *Don Quixote* is that it fails many of the critical and consumer tests of our literary culture, a culture in the grips of a narrow, bland definition of what constitutes a good book.

The Czech novelist Milan Kundera believes the legacy of *Don Quixote* has been denigrated by an adherence to the "imperative of verisimilitude" in the novel. He lays partial blame on our fixation with realistic settings and chronological order. Douglas Glover qualifies Kundera by suggesting that literary realism is a technique which becomes problematic only when "someone tries to turn it into a definition." Glover admits, however, that this is precisely what "unthinking writers and journalist-critics" have done. Psychological realism, with its emphasis on credible plots and believable characters, is a major tradition in western literature. But it isn't the only one.

In 2003 the Observer newspaper published a list of the hundred greatest novels. The books are presented chronologically, starting with *Don Quixote* and ending with *Austerlitz*, by W.G. Sebald, published in 2002. Only eight of the titles pre-date Jane Austen and more than sixty selected books were written in the last century. A scan of the list validates Milan Kundera's concern about the dominance of the realistic novel. The eighteenth century took Miguel de Cervantes' adventurous spirit to heart. The age's essential works, including *Robinson Crusoe* by Daniel Defoe (published in 1719, and often credited as the first English novel), Jonathan Swift's *Gulliver's Travels* (1725) and *Tom Jones* by Henry Fielding (1746), share with *Don Quixote* an unscripted, spontaneous quality that translates into surprises on nearly every page.

With Laurence Sterne's *Tristram Shandy* (1759-67), the century had its masterpiece, a hilarious, often unbuttoned work that Kundera praises for its philosophical and aesthetic "lightness." "What is all this story about?" cries an exasperated Sterne character. The answer is a "COCK and a BULL," and it is "one of the best of its kind, I ever heard."

But once beyond *Tristram Shandy* the Observer tracks the steady ascendancy of psychological realism. Standing as a counterpoint to nineteenth-century titans like Dickens, Thackeray, Balzac and Stendhal are the modestly quixotic efforts *Alice's Adventures in Wonderland* by Lewis Carroll (1870) and Kenneth Graham's 1908 *The Wind in the Willows*. Though twentieth-century modernism shared Miguel de Cervantes' ardour for innovation, Joyce's *Ulysses* (1922) and *USA* by John Dos Passos (1933) strike many today as chilly Olympian exercises in expanding the form, not to mention exhausting the reader. Among recent titles, Martin Amis's *Money* (1983), with its Cervantes-like cameos by the author, and *Wise Children* by Angela Carter (1986) possess the familiar flair and self-awareness, as does Milan Kundera's own *The Book of Laughter and Forgetting* (1984).

Should the Observer list be updated, a twenty-first century novel in the Quixote mode might just make the cut. It unfolds an outlandish yarn about a boy trapped in a lifeboat with a tiger, and promises to tell a story that will make readers believe in God. Yann Martel's *Life of Pi*, first published in 2001, has been rightly lauded for its originality. The book's *zeitgeist* plea for tolerance, especially its blending of three great faiths – Hinduism, Christianity, and Islam – in the character of Pi Patel, has also been a natural focus of attention. Literary novels are rarely both the news that never goes out of fashion and the lead story of the day.

Less often remarked is that *Life of Pi* has an old soul. Daniel Defoe would have cheered the boy's adventures at sea. Jonathan Swift might have nodded approval at the flesh-eating island where Pi nearly meets a grisly end. Laurence Sterne could have offered Cock-and-Bull advice to Martel about his narrative strategy of demanding we accept the ever taller tales he presents, by way of literally proving the novel's contention that humans believe in God because it is, in effect, the better story.

And Cervantes? He'd have appreciated the conflicting explanations for what happened to Pi during those months adrift on the ocean, and Martel's decision to leave the choice up to us. The sense of discovery, of stories and questions being invitations to tell more stories and ask more questions, would have likewise pleased the Spaniard. Then there is the final sentence in the author's note. "If we, citizens, do not support our artists," Yann Martel writes, "then we sacrifice our imagination on the altar of crude reality and we end up believing in nothing and having worthless dreams." Don Quixote himself might have proclaimed such a defiant, fool-hearty sentiment.

The success of *Life of Pi* – three million copies sold in some forty countries – may be testament to the latent appeal of narrative enchantment. Novels, it is worth repeating, simply aren't true to life. They are always fictions and always invitations to set off on an imaginative quest. That quest is to discover, or perhaps simply be reminded of, what is essential to our natures – i.e. the 'reality' of being human. There is the deeper irony to our voluntary imprisonment in literary verisimilitude. "In our fictional universe," Douglas Glover concludes, "books teach us to be real."

"This is how the book begins," Barbara Nichol teaches future adult readers at the start of *Tales of Don Quixote*. The story is about the hero "Don Quixote – an ordinary man who thinks he is a knight," and the author "writing his big book about his hero." When *Don Quixote* was first published, Nichol admits, it was a surprise to people, "not like any books they'd read before." That was four hundred years ago. "And even now, literature is borrowing ideas from Cervantes and trying to catch up."

2005

A CIVILIZING INFLUENCE:

Tariq Ali's Islam Quintet

A shame, really, that no one thought to publish *How The Muslims Saved Civilization* back in the 1990s. Such a book might have outlined the debt owed by the great minds of the sixteenth-century Renaissance to Islamic scholarship, especially in astronomy, medicine, and math. Or the earlier bequeathment to medieval Europe of versions of Aristotle, Plato, and Euclid, courtesy of Muslim translators working in Moorish Spain. Or any of the other influences and encounters in what historian Steven Runciman has called "the long sequence of interaction and fusion between Orient and Occident." *How The Muslims Saved Civilization* would surely have been welcomed by readers a decade ago, just as they welcomed Thomas Cahill's 1995 account of heroic Irish monks who performed similar good deeds.

Unless, that is, something about linking Muslims with civilization in the title would have caused confusion. Admirers of Cahill's *How The Irish Saved Civilization* knew that, by the term "civilization," the American scholar meant the recorded greatness of Greece and Rome, which was preserved by Irish scribes until Europe could climb out of its dark age and become civilized again. No offence was intended against the cultures of India or China or any other corner of the globe where, in effect, little of this history applied. This was the rise and fall and rise again of white Europe.

Would a book title in which Muslims, whose skin is generally less white and who are associated today with North Africa and the Middle and Far East, were proclaimed to have also played a role in the resurgence of Western civilization have been readily understood? Explaining that large numbers of followers of Islam once lived and flourished in places such as Spain and Sicily might have helped. The city of Granada featured Muslim public baths in most

125

neighbourhoods? Residents of twelfth-century Salerno could have counted a hundred mosques inside their city walls?

Regardless, September 11, 2001, put an end to soft book ideas. Since the twin towers fell, the times have demanded blunt tomes with aggressive titles and subtitles that could, in different hands, double as recruitment slogans for one jihad or another. Historian Bernard Lewis's *What Went Wrong* and *The Crisis of Islam* have swollen to bestsellerdom in part, one suspects, on the inflammatory nature of their monikers. If Lewis has any regrets about the names chosen, it may be because the real banner he wished to run across both dust jackets – the now-axiomatic "clash of civilizations," which he coined in an earlier essay – was usurped by Samuel Huntington for his more nuanced *The Clash of Civilizations and the Remaking of the World Order*. Lewis has had to be content with subtitles that are locked and loaded: *The Clash Between Islam and Modernity in the Middle East* and *Holy War and Unholy Terror* respectively.

Forget some waffling about forgotten cultural interactions and shared ancestries. The only acceptable narrative at present is the conflict between civilizations, one modern and righteous and the other in the throes of the terror and crisis that comes from being, so to speak, wrong. This may be a largely rhetorical clash, but when oppositional forces meet, whether in reality or the media, the noise can be deafening. Among those publishing at maximum volume since 9/11 has been the historian and essayist Tariq Ali. Both his *The Clash of Fundamentalisms: Crusades, Jihads and Modernity* and *Bush in Babylon: The Recolonization of Iraq* give from the international Left at least as good as they get from the American Right.

But that same Tariq Ali has also nearly completed the sort of quiet writing project seemingly out of step with our loud age. *A Sultan in Palermo* is the fourth volume in the Islam Quintet, a series of historical novels that probe the lengthy encounter between Islam and Western Christendom. The series is revisionist in impulse, wishing to suggest that the dominant history of Europe in the last millennium, if not quite the lie told by the winner, as Napoleon Bonaparte once remarked, has certainly involved obscuring the truth about those who "lost" the continent. "If things go on like this," a character says at the start of the first novel, *Shadows of the*

Pomegranate Tree, "nothing will be left of us except a fragrant memory."

The quintet opens in 1499, in al-Andalus. Queen Isabella is solidifying the reconquista of the land that Christians call Spain from the dark-skinned heathens who have been occupying parts of it for six centuries. Amid the slaughters, expulsions, and conversions-by-inquisition, one act of savagery stands out. Ximenes de Cisneros, the Catholic archbishop in charge of the dirty work, has sent soldiers into the libraries and private homes with book collections around the city of Granada, ordering that all Arab-language titles be collected for burning. Like many such gestures, Cisneros' involves a backhanded compliment: these people care enough about books to be devastated by their loss.

Indeed, among the texts are several thousand copies of the Koran, many exquisitely crafted, along with "rare manuscripts vital to the entire architecture of intellectual life in al-Andalus." The collection is both a testament to the sophistication of Moorish Spain and the envy of scholars in the rest of Europe. The priest is convinced that Muslims can be eliminated as a force in the Iberian Peninsula only if their culture is erased. He signals the torchbearers to light the bonfire, then listens, unmoved, as helpless onlookers offer their faith's timeless assertion of fidelity: "There is only one Allah and he is Allah and Mohammed is his Prophet."

Moorish Spain, as embodied by the fictional aristocratic clan, the Banu Hudayl, whose mansion outside Granada was first constructed in AD 935, three years after the family left Damascus for the western outpost of Islam, is about to be eradicated. Literally nothing and no one will survive the fanaticism of the overlords, who are, by the by, primitive by comparison with those they exterminate. The last survivor of the Hudayls, an eleven-year-old child, has a knife plunged into his chest by a sociopathic teenage army captain. The epilogue, which jumps ahead twenty years, further darkens this compelling, if not always seamless, first effort at rendering history through narrative. The captain, revealed as Cortés, is shown entering the great city of Tenochtitlan, or present-day Mexico City, where king Moctezuma is naively waiting to greet him.

By beginning in Spain, *Shadows of the Pomegranate Tree* goes straight for the geographical heart of Muslim grievances about their legacy in Europe. Ali may have chosen al-Andalus as his inaugural canvas because the story is reasonably well-known, especially the bonfire at Granada. His decision with the next volume, *The Book of Saladin*, to shift three centuries back to the region from which the Hudayl family originally fled, suggests a twofold ambition for the series. First impressions of the early novels are likely to focus on their portraits of Islamic societies in Mediterranean Europe. These sketches, vivid and warm without being idealized, have the freshness of images recently discovered beneath the paint of other representations. Much of the pleasure of reading Ali's fiction lies in his detailing of daily life, both high and low, and daily appetites, including sexual and culinary. As a novelist, he is possessed with a fine historical intelligence and a storytelling impulse that owes as much to Arabian Nights as it does to Tolstoy. Admirers of tales replete with scheming eunuchs and harem intrigues, women of complex lusts, and men who love women and men alike, won't be disappointed.

But a more cerebral ambition underpins how history unfolds in the books. When lined up beside each other, the novels compare and contrast the fates of these societies. As well as excavating the secret Islamicization of Europe, Ali is posing a question: why did Islam, once so pluralistic and intellectually progressive, ossify and withdraw to such a degree that it wound up isolated from the continent it helped civilize? In Moorish Spain, he identifies the force and animosity of external enemies as the principal cause. In other cases, the fault is largely internal.

The Book of Saladin finds the culture at perhaps the peak of its achievements. Salah al-Din, or Saladin, the legendary Kurdish Sultan of Syria and Egypt, arrives at the Cairo house of the Jewish scholar Ibn Yakub, who he hires as his personal scribe. Though Jerusalem was lost to the Christians in the First Crusade of 1099, Saladin's rule over the cities of Cairo and Damascus has allowed for the evolution of an urban civilization far in advance of anything in continental Europe. His caliphate is also tolerant, welcoming Jews and Christians to dwell alongside Believers. All are People of the Book, sharing much of the Old and New Testament and many of the prophets. Saladin himself is revered for his generosity and fairness: a good ruler, as rare in the Islamic world as anywhere else.

The Sultan's vow to retake Jerusalem, known to Arabs as al-Kuds, is within his military reach so long as he can maintain unity among his emirs. History records Saladin recapturing the city in 1187, only to be confronted by still another wave of crusaders, including the English King Richard the Lionhearted. Ostensibly the victor in the Third Crusade as well, Saladin was worn down equally by battles with Christians and with his own fractious tribes. History also records that Islam did not achieve prominence again in the Holy Land until the rise of the Ottomans centuries later.

Making the boldest time leap in the series, *The Stone Woman* bypasses the glorious days of the final Islamic empire to meditate on its long twilight. The novel, which details the story of a disaffected Turkish aristocrat named Nilofer who returns to her family home outside Istanbul in 1899, is a Chekhovian exercise in philosophical sighs and political inertia. Characters squander afternoons lamenting the retreat of the Ottoman Empire from the Europe that emerged out of the Renaissance. "Istanbul," one character remarks, "could have been the capital of invention and modernity like Cordoba and Baghdad in the old days, but these wretched beards that established the laws of our state were frightened of losing their monopoly of power and knowledge." The "beards" are the conservative clergy, who had, for instance, persuaded one sixteenth-century sultan that the printing press would be a threat to stability. Another character summarizes the sentiment among the family: "I think our decline is well deserved."

With its purposeful inactivity and daring foray into the mind of a Muslim woman, *The Stone Woman* is a striking counterpoint to the bustle of the other books, foreshadowing the condition of Islam still another century into its crisis. "Everything is being taken away and nothing is ready to take its place," Nilofer warns her children. "It is this that turns many ordinary people into madmen and assassins."

Such prophesy could well have compelled a fourth volume that actualized Nilofer's darkest worries for 1999 or beyond. Instead, *A Sultan in Palermo* swings back to the twelfth century, this time in Sicily. First conquered by Arabs in 827, the island was retaken by the

Normans in 1091. The majority Muslim population benefited, however, from a ruler, Roger II, who so admired Islam that he both adopted its customs and kept his less-admiring barons in check. As in Moorish Spain and the Damascus of Saladin, the Palermo of the "baptized Sultan" is a multicultural court in which Muslims, Jews, and Nazarenes live and work together. For Ali, these periods of fruitful coexistence are to be noted. History in the quintet isn't a force above and beyond human agency. Civilizations don't clash; only individuals do, and they can always resolve otherwise.

A Sultan in Palermo is the first volume to appear since 9/11. For the most part, the book is unaffected by the rising screech of debate in journalism and non-fiction. The tale of the efforts of al-Idrisi, a court scholar and adviser to Roger II, to stave off the disaster of his ruler's impending death keeps pace in both plot and detail with *The Book of Saladin*, the finest of the novels so far. That a scholar should fail to stop the Normans from slaughtering Muslims after a change in leadership, thus initiating the erasure of Islam in Sicily, is no surprise: the leisurely wind-down of the Ottoman Empire is a luxury afforded to few Arabs in Europe. Extinction was more the norm.

Only Ali's portrait of the historic figure of al-Idrisi betrays what may be a post-9/11 frustration with the ways that novels go about revealing truth. When not struggling to save his people or having sex five times in one night with his wife's sister (called the "Five Obligations"), the fifty-eight year old is pondering scientific and political advances not due to occur for hundreds of years. These include the theories of gravity and natural selection, and the Marxist plan for the fair distribution of land among peasants. He even offers tips on healthy eating.

Idrisi is, in short, a Super Arab, and had T-shirts been the fashion in medieval Sicily, he might have had one printed with "Muslims Do It Better." This mild lapse into the megaphone rhetoric of our age, while forgivable given the author's engagement with politics in addition to literature, should still be cautioned. Even partisan fiction can't survive too much cheerleading. More important, it is precisely the reserved, measured truths about humanity contained within the Islam Quintet that we "People of the Book" need to be reading right now.

There is a riddle yet to be answered by the series. To date, Tariq Ali has balanced stories that explore European Islamic societies destroyed by external forces with those brought down by their own internal failings. As such, the fifth novel could be expected to either tip the balance or propose a new dynamic. My guess is that Ali may finally plunge into the early twentieth century, possibly the Palestine of fading empires and competing needs and agendas. Here, too, he would find a Muslim society at risk of obliteration, and rulers mostly weak but occasionally strong, and instances of clash and co-operation alike, and more than a few passionate individuals who, though determined not to become fragrant memories, may still end up forgotten, history being what it is.

2005

BURNING MAN:

Pankaj Mishra In The World

Suppose for a moment that we really are in crisis. Suppose, too, the crisis is located not so much in the latest terrorist atrocity or misguided invasion as inside our hearts and minds. It lies within the very notions of who we are, which we have constructed and now cannot sustain. The crisis is the self and, to paraphrase one orange-robed sage, the whole edifice is a house on fire.

The proposition will strike most North Americans as plain silly. For hundreds of years, the autonomous self has been the engine of Western civilization, as well as a model for the rest of the planet. Once, medieval Europe had bound identity to clan, church, and king. People were who they belonged to, the sums of their relationships and obligations. With the dissolution of that form of life came "the plunge into the adventure of individuality," as Pankaj Mishra describes it in *An End to Suffering: The Buddha in the World*. A new vocabulary for human character evolved during the Enlightenment and Industrial Age, one that emphasized "personal choice and desire and the capacity for self-transformation." Fresh configurations of nations and economies followed, designed both to encourage and regulate competing self-interests. Ambitions for liberty and prosperity became good for your country, good for you. One newborn state went so far as to declare the pursuit of happiness a democratic right. What an idea.

The twentieth century exported this "secular assessment of human possibility" into regions of the globe where it had had virtually no historic foothold. India was a major point of contact, along with China and the rest of Asia, and it was in this country – or in the version of it bequeathed by Prime Minister Jawaharlal Nehru – that Mishra, a thirty-five year old with an ancient soul and a transgressive intellect, was raised. Here was another young republic that promised its poorest and most downtrodden citizens happiness as European-style rational individuals. Secular education and socialist economic systems, as envisioned by Nehru and his successors, would induce an emboldened India full of individuals empowered to pursue their every private need and desire, even though, as Mishra notes, the notion had "hardly any precedents in India's own intellectual and spiritual traditions." This was not, after all, the land of Adam Smith or Karl Marx but, rather, of Mahatma Gandhi and, further back still, Siddhartha Gautama, better known as the Buddha.

An End to Suffering, a singular cross of biography, memoir, and essay, traverses East and West and back again to gather evidence about the nature of our global predicament. Though Mishra's debut novel, *The Romantics*, published in 1999, suggested a serious talent, his reputation is still based more on his work as a literary essayist and traveller to troubled places. Journeys taken over the past decade into Afghanistan, Pakistan, and Kashmir first alerted him to the legions of mostly young men for whom the fantasy of modernity, of a future where everyone would "wear a tie, work in an office or factory, practise birth control, raise a nuclear family, drive a car and pay taxes," was collapsing in disappointment. Fundamentalism offered these men an alternative fantasy, the one starring jihad warriors and suicide bombers in the roles of martyrs.

Then came September 11, and the appearance, at least, of a global clash. *An End to Suffering* has wisdom to offer about the present state of affairs. But the book's radical proposal involves applying the teachings of an Indian prince-turned-sage who died more than twenty-four hundred years ago. Pankaj Mishra recommends the Buddha despite knowing that Gautama can be relied upon to make two very contrary, and somewhat baffling, assertions.

The first is that, as usual, the crisis isn't the one you thought it was – i.e., some external circumstance impeding the universe from unfolding as it should. The problem, rather, is you: the prison of your desires and the illusion of your identity, with its false imperative to achieve some pressing destiny. And the only lasting solution? This is the second assertion, and it is still more astonishing, especially to Western ears. Get out of that metaphorical burning house, the Buddha advises. Out of what? Nothing less than your own presumed-to-be stable self. Get out of it, and quickly.

Buddhism, a friend likes to joke, is religion for accountants. There are the Three Fires and Four Noble Truths, the Five Bundles of Personality and Ten Fetters. The Noble Eightfold Path, which proceeds from the final truth, offers a bonus Threefold Plan of Action. Contained within the twelve links of the Chain of Dependent Causation are terms that are, Karen Armstrong acknowledges in her recent biography, *Buddha*, difficult to even understand, let alone put into practice. If the Eightfold Path to enlightenment is less daunting, be grateful for its use of repetition: the Right View, Right Intention, Right Speech, and so on.

The lists, which Armstrong dutifully unscrolls in her straightforward account of the prince who became the lotus sage and the legends from Indian antiquity that cohered into a great Asian philosophy, do serve a purpose. The Buddha was a teacher and preacher alike, and his audience was almost certainly illiterate. (Among the many things not known about the real Gautama was whether he could read.) Lists aid memorization. They also encourage thinking in terms of process, as when following a manual. The Ten Commandments aside, Christianity can't touch Buddhism when it comes to columns of edicts and advice. Nor can any other religion manage the same appeal to our own itemizing era, with its fondness for twelve-step programs and *Seven Habits of Highly Successful People*.

In Srinivas Krishna's film *Masala*, two Hindu deities, slumming it as human beings, are about to crash an airplane. "Thank God, we are Gods," one quips to the other. But while Hinduism, Greek mythology, Judaism and Christianity feature all-powerful gods, the Buddha was having none of this Higher Being business. His business was about being human, and he had zero patience for doctrines concerning hierarchies or ultimate reality. He had, in fact, no real theology to impart or philosophy to share. Rather, his fussy lists sketched out, in Mishra's words, a "medical diagnosis and cure" for suffering that was both psychologically acute and ethical.

Negative emotions such as anger, hatred, malice, and jealousy, are caused by a false attachment to such seemingly rock-solid entities as the self and the phenomenal world. A sense of identity isn't so much problematic as delusional. We don't exist as autonomous beings, despite what our insatiable hungers and thirsts suggest. Instead, we are part of a complex flow of phenomena in a universe at once impermanent and beyond our control. The Greek philosopher Heraclitus, a near contemporary of Gautama, had a similar idea: "You cannot step into the same river twice."

Understanding that impermanence, and the interconnectedness it implies, brings more than release from individual suffering and disappointment. It helps one become a more disciplined person. There is a reason why the Buddha is forever depicted in solitary repose, eyes cast downward. He doesn't offer a weekly service, let alone a sermon bracketed by hymns. His treatment certainly doesn't feature healing circles or group hugs. Giving over to one's desires, or to the authority of a state or even a God, represents a retreat from personal responsibility. You, and you alone, must regulate your mind. You, and you alone, must liberate your actions. A "private remedy for private distress," is Mishra's elegant summary, multiplied by six billion.

Both *An End to Suffering* and *Buddha* are careful to locate this still singular idea – a challenge, Pankaj Mishra grants, to the "very basis of conventional human self-perceptions" – in the Buddha's own lifetime. Sixth-century BC India saw the breakdown of smaller societies and older moralities, and their replacement with the tumult of emerging empires. Traditional consolations of faith and community were vanishing. People feared for their personal security, and for the future. "Terror, awe and dread," is how one Buddhist scripture summarized the mood.

That was then. But that is now as well, amid what Mishra calls the "great violence and confusion" of the present day. The young Indian casts a cold eye on what the West has sought to impose upon the rest of the planet. Some of his pronouncements seem almost calculated to inflame. He dismisses the individual of the European model as a creature living "merely for the sake of increasing and satisfying his material needs." He also declares nearly everything in the modern world to be "predicated on the growth and multiplication of desire."

Mishra's trenchant conclusion is this: the political and social arrangements that our autonomous selves have rendered tyrannical must be overcome. The Buddha offers a regimen that can liberate us from the burning house of our unappeasable selves. He outlines a kind of spiritual politics that demands human beings accept responsibility for their actions and, having been made aware of the interdependency of individuals and societies, behave with compassion and kindness. The flight from individuality will be tough going – our flawed, self-regarding natures, while being a cause of suffering, may also, Mishra admits, be a source of vitality – but the effort alone can constitute the closest thing possible to an ethical life, as well as an antidote to the fanaticism spreading like a pox across the globe.

Geography may be destiny here. While *An End to Suffering* boldly circles the planet of ideas, it sticks physically close to the small patch where Siddhartha Gautama walked the earth. Not so coincidentally, that patch also contains the majority of the author's own footsteps. In both cases, it is the India not of the mystical Himalayas, as the popular imagination would favour – Buddhism migrated north to Tibet only in the seventh century – but of the dusty, crowded plains of the Ganges basin. There, unkempt sages and seers wandered the roads begging alms and seeking wisdom, or just escape. They did so in 483 BC, the year of the Buddha's death, and they still do in 2004 AD, the year George Bush is re-elected. As Pankaj Mishra researches his subject, he charts the emergence of his own unsatisfactory self amid the exhausted rice fields and villages of mud and straw, where, he writes, "the feeling of being exposed in the vast flatland never leaves you." Thus do philosophies of being spring from a specific physical setting into the universal consciousness of women and men.

Pop-Buddhism tends to play down its roots in the Asian subcontinent, fearing, perhaps, the severity of that ancestry for those who simply wish to dabble, without ever feeling so exposed. It's good to be reminded that such fearsome therapy for the problems of being alive emerged from a place where existence is not easily maintained, and where questions about the fundamentals are asked with the same regularity as queries about the weather. In the end, Richard Gere or even Leonard Cohen can't help you much with this point, although lines from Cohen's song "Boogie Street" come close to capturing the lay of that distinctive landscape: "So come, my friend, be not afraid/We are so lightly here/It is in love that we are made/In love we disappear."

* * *

In one scene in *Temptations of the West: How to be Modern in India, Pakistan, Tibet, and Beyond*, Pankaj Mishra finds himself in a hillside town in Kashmir, the Himalayan valley positioned so disastrously between the warring politics of India and Pakistan. He has travelled there to investigate a fire that destroyed a shrine to a 15th-century patron-saint. Having talked to locals and noted the destitution, he prepares to leave.

"Word of my presence in the town had quickly spread," he writes. Sure enough, a delegation of about forty men appears. They have walked four miles from a still more remote place to meet Mishra, hoping that he is an official who can help get a burst pipe repaired. Their village has been without water for eight days. They are running out of snow to melt.

"Raggedly dressed," he notes of the delegation, "large holes gaping from their pherans, their thickly bearded faces white with dust, they seemed to have emerged out of an eighteenth- or nineteenth-century wretchedness." He listens patiently, if helplessly, to their complaints.

The encounter captures core qualities of Mishra's journalism. This gifted Indian is the author of the novel, *The Romantics*, as well as the extraordinary non-fiction work *An End to Suffering: the Buddha in the World*. He is also a regular contributor to publications in England and the United States, including *The New York Times* and *The New York Review of Books*. His writing is marked by fearlessness and freshness alike, and his equal ease with the intellectual traditions of East and West allows for often pioneering forays across various divides.

He is, as it happens, also a bearded local man who could easily be confused in Kashmir – or Kabul or Kathmandu – for an official with expertise in burst pipes. The son of a railway employee from the Brahmin caste, Pankaj Mishra was raised in a series of provincial towns with the same vague hopes as millions of his generation: a career in the civil service and a life somehow exempted from the "ordinary misery and degradation of India." Though still in his thirties, the author has, in effect, already journeyed greater distances, both geographic and psychological, than do most people in the course of a lifetime.

As such, he is uniquely positioned to recognize and understand men and women who are, as he puts it in *Temptations of the West*, "lured away from their subsistence economies and abandoned on the threshold of a world in which they found they had, and could have, no place." The same applies to nations obliged to "join the modern world and find new identities" in often dire, bloody circumstances. These preoccupations direct Mishra's travels across the Indian subcontinent. Besides India, where he still lives for part of the year, he visits, generally more than once, Pakistan and Afghanistan, Nepal and Tibet.

The book follows narrative roads that other journalists might not be able to locate on maps. Charting the ominous racial "project of a Hindu nation" in his homeland, Mishra talks to everyone from politicians to gangsters to amalgams like Ramchandra Paramhans, the godfather of Hindu nationalism. "Two bodyguards nervously watched my face as Paramhans described this history," he writes of this encounter with an old man who had recently been the target of assassins.

In another tense moment, Mishra winds through the slums of Allahabad to meet a politician who represents the Dalits, a term for the various low castes in India, including the Untouchable. In the man's house he is stared down by supporters, who likely recognize him as a Brahmin. "It occurred to me," he writes, noticing the young men's scrutiny of his clothes and shoes, "that I was the only fully dressed person there."

Back in Kashmir, Mishra chases the story of a massacre of Sikh villagers, despite that reaching the village involves negotiating army roadblocks. Confessing his fear, he grants that "far too many journalists investigating strange events in remote parts of Kashmir had been killed."

His reportage of the massacre is typically vivid. Sikh men were "shouting, beating their chests, feeding upon each other's energy." The sound of weeping women was causing roosters to "go on dementedly for several hours after dawn, their exultant cries hanging discordantly above the village." This scene, too, seems to belong in another age.

Pankaj Mishra is no less intrepid in his travels through Afghanistan, both under the Taliban and during the present period. Uneasy with the presence of the international aid community, and wary that the country could still fail, due to the re-emergence of drug cartels, he wonders at the load-bearing capacity of what is essentially a premodern societal structure. "The obstinacy and destructiveness of the

Taliban now appear part of the history of Afghanistan's calamitous encounter with the modern world," he says.

But then, calamitous encounters appear the fate of much of the planet these days, due, in no small part, to those temptations mentioned in the title. "Western ideologies," Mishra argues in his preface, be they colonialism, communism or globalization, demand that nations "modernize or perish." The resulting pressures can be overwhelming, for countries and their beleaguered citizens alike. Nor does slowing the pace seem an option.

Were *Temptations of the West* simply a collection of travel essays that ponders how places like India and Nepal negotiate a globalized planet, it would still be a fine book. But the intensity of Mishra's prose suggests that he wants the disruption, and the upheaval, to be felt viscerally. Daring reportage, and an empathy for ordinary people, goes some way towards this ambition.

As important, though, is the use of his own narrative as evidence of the "bewildering complexity" faced by individuals swept along by those negotiations. If, as he claims, the movement for one traveller at least was from "ignorance and prejudice to a measure of self-awareness and knowledge," then it might prove the same for certain readers. Great books, and great books only, can have that rare effect.

2004/2006

ALL SEX IS REAL:

The Mainstreaming Of Pornography

In 2003, porn actor Ron Jeremy made a tour of American college campuses. At every stop the veteran of 1,800 hard-core films was greeted by fans, many of them teenagers. Few who clamoured to see Jeremy had likely rented his 1987 movie *21 Hump Street* or 1996's *Another White Trash Whore*. They knew him instead through the reality-TV show *The Surreal Life* and documentary *Porn Star – The Legend of Ron Jeremy*, as well as his cameos in Hollywood films like *The Rules of Attraction* and *Boogie Nights*. At the University of Alabama Jeremy participated in one of a series of debates with the Canadian author and anti-porn activist Susan G. Cole. As reported in Pamela Paul's *Pornified*, students in attendance, some wearing 'I love porn' T-shirts, cheered Jeremy's boasts of the benefits of pornography and "having a party" while booing Cole for her objections. "What's your fucking problem?" one young scholar asked Cole during the question period.

Pornography, it is worth remembering, peeled off its brown-paper wrapping only quite recently. The way it struts through popular culture these days, waving various small flags of faux liberation and a much larger banner bearing a simple dollar sign, you might think it had gone mainstream back in the 1960s, along with the pill. In fact, the porn parade down the boulevards of North American life is about a decade old, and many middle-aged watchers, unschooled in *sex.com* or Britney Spears, still may not be sure what those raunchy floats and teenage pole dancers represent. Younger observers, having grown up inside the Net, and anyone attempting to raise children in the early twenty-first century know all too well.

The clever industry fluttering of those lesser flags – pornography as sexual liberation, as third-wave feminist assertion, as freedom of expression battleground – in the faces of concern seemed to temporarily stifle commentaries. For a pioneering group of critics and

141

novelists, the wish is to remark not on the spectrum of porn that reflects a liberated relationship with sex, but those activities that are symptomatic of a distorted and even abusive vision of human sexuality. Distinguishing the exhibitionist tendencies of giggly college girls from, say, dubiously consensual incest websites out of Eastern Europe ought to be easy enough. But extreme porn, especially the degraded forms that flourish in cyberspace, invites both conflations and a tendency to moralize.

Moral objections, however, more than legal or aesthetic ones, may be the most instinctive response to what Martin Amis calls "the obscenification of everyday life." Harm, observers are asserting, is being done here. Harm to those watching extreme porn and harm, for certain, to those being watched. Harm as well to community standards, especially those concerning young people, who still deserve our protection and guidance. Finally, harm is being done to all our fragile sexual selves, which may not be able to withstand the relentless assaults of a billion dollar industry committed less to providing erotic pleasure than to making a mess of our relationships with each other.

Ariel Levy began noticing the change several years ago. The author of *Female Chauvinist Pigs* would switch on her television to find "strippers in pasties explaining how best to lap dance a man to orgasm." Viewing the film *Charlie's Angels*, a hit the summer of 2000, she would juxtapose the assertions of its stars that they were presenting strong women with the visual evidence of the actresses dressing on screen in "alternating soft-porn styles." On the newsstands were fresh examples of the "porny new genre" dubbed the "lad magazine." Publications such as *Maxim*, *FHM*, and *Stuff* fixated on "greased celebrities in little scraps of fabric humping the floor."

Equally, the thirty-year-old New York journalist, whose mother attended weekly women's consciousness-raising groups and didn't own any makeup, was observing teenage girls walking the streets in jeans that exposed their "butt cleavage" and tops showing "breast implants and pierced navels alike." Those women were, moreover, cheerfully stripping for the "Girls Gone Wild" videos. They were also going to strip clubs and buying the memoirs of porn stars Jenna Jameson and Traci Lords, both of whom graced the *New York Times* bestseller list. "When I was in porn," Lords admitted in 2003, "it was like a back-alley thing. Now it's everywhere."

How, Levy wanted to learn, had the "tawdry, tarty, cartoon-like version of female sexuality" of a Pamela Anderson or Paris Hilton come to be not merely ubiquitous but promoted as a marker of the advances of women in a post-feminist world? "Because we have determined that all empowered women must be overtly and publicly sexual," she writes, "and because the only sign of sexuality we seem able to recognize is a direct allusion to red-light entertainment, we have laced the sleazy energy and aesthetic of a topless club or a *Penthouse* shoot throughout our culture." Barbara Walters interviewed Hilton for her 2004 "most fascinating people of the year" program.

"Raunch culture," as Levy calls it, may be hardest on adolescent and teenaged girls. Blitzed with images of how to be "hot," young people, already prone to insecurities, have a difficult time distinguishing the fake from the real. Their mothers, at least, could summon an era when the politics of feminism were still ascendant. Not so their new-millennium daughters. "They have never known a time when 'ho' wasn't part of the lexicon," she contends, "when sixteen-year-olds didn't get breast implants." Nor do most teens yet possess the sense of irony needed to negotiate a cynical, commerce-driven pop culture. This is their reality, and too often they accept it at its false-face value.

If Andrea Levy offers a PG-13 critique of the mainstreaming of pornography, *Pornified* heads with grim determination for the XXX shelves – or, better, the websites. "Porn.Inc," Pamela Paul points out, has evolved from a $10-million business in 1975, flashing its wares in selected grotty movie houses around the United States, into a $13-billion industry in 2004. While a few porn palaces yet blink their come-ons and all but a fraction of the pay-per-view movie sales in hotels are "adult" in content, and while Americans did rent 800 million sex videos last year, in addition to spending $4 billion buying these movies for home use; still, it is the digital proliferation of porn through the internet where the colossal profits are to be made. In Paul's view, Internet porn is also where the lasting damage is being done.

"Old school defenders of pornography," she writes, "may not be familiar with the direction in which Internet and DVD-era pornography has gone." When an entertainment analyst is asked to define "acceptable adult programming" for specialty cable TV, his list includes penetration, oral, anal, and group sex, along with lesbian and gay sex. Such material, the analyst admits, "used to be called pornography, but a lot of that has become socially acceptable now." What is pornographic these days? The bar, needless to say, especially in cyber-porn, has nowhere to go but down. "Pregnant women become pornified," Paul reports of her own journalistic exploration of this realm, "their naked torsos wrested from personal websites onto "pregnant porn" websites, incest becomes fetishized, child pornography blends with adult pornography into an ageless "teen porn" middle ground. Any sense of taboo dissipates in a free-for-all porn world."

Much of *Pornified* is devoted to cyber-porn addiction. Her broad focus is on men and boys, by far the biggest junkies. Interviewing American males with names like Harrison, Gabe, and Ian, Pamela Paul learns how obsessive cruising of the Net wreaks havoc on their conceptions of women and sexuality. They become impatient with their partners and grow numb to the pleasures of conventional sex. "Pornography leaves men desensitized to both outrage and to excitement," she says, leading to dissatisfaction with the emotional tugs of their own lives. By definition, addicts crave more junk. With cyber-porn those cravings encourage greater expansion of the global "pornotopia": more gonzo group-sex sites from Russia, wilder teen stuff from Japan. Addiction, the book argues, fuels the extremity. Debasement, in turn, deepens the addiction.

In her determination to establish an accelerated continuum of damage, Paul too easily conflates distinct varieties of porn. She also fails to erect a clear enough divide between these pursuits and the illness – and criminality – of child pornography. Likewise, the hot rage that underscores the book's cool reportage occasionally blinds it to certain eternal truths. All the practices she lists, for instance, and many more besides, exist in late nineteenth-century pornographic photography. Nor, sadly, was the creation of, and trading in, sexual imagery involving minors born with the Internet. On a more banal note, while the woeful tales of Harrison, Gabe, and Ian are illustrative, they may not reveal any pathology exclusive to the consumption of pornography. Harrison, Gabe, and Ian, or men just like them, are probably always going to be addicted to something, and always harming those nearest to them with their addictions.

For all its moral outrage, *Pornified* advocates a tempered "censure-not-censor" response, the aim being to move society away from viewing pornography as "hip and fun and sexy" and toward recognizing it as "harmful, pathetic, and decidedly unsexy." Its author may simply have spent too much time on the Net for her own good. Here, one suspects, is the Rubicon none of us should seek to cross. What cyber-porn permits isn't so much boundless tawdry choice and glum stimulation as too effortless an absolution from the reality of what is being observed. Flickering across a million monitors in a hundred countries at this very moment are tales less of *Debbie Doing Dallas* or *Just Another White Trash Whore* than of women and men performing acts before a camera because they are poor, or damaged, or even have been coerced. It shouldn't be so easy not to think about this while pleasing ourselves through their bodies.

Pamela Paul does not include sex-industry workers in her survey. Though Ariel Levy refers to them only briefly, she does observe as a "cliché that bears repeating" that most women who make sex films were themselves the victims of sexual abuse. Based on conversations with experts, and too freely lumping prostitutes with porn actresses of all schools, she puts the figure at between 65 and 90 percent. She also cites a 1998 study titled "Prostitution in Five Countries: Violence and Post-Traumatic Stress Disorder." It concludes that two-thirds of sex workers suffer from symptoms identical to those of post-traumatic stress disorder – twice the percentage as of American soldiers returning from the war in Vietnam. "There is something twisted about using a predominantly sexually traumatized group of people as our role models," she says, thinking perhaps of Jenna Jameson, whose book *How to Make Love like a Porn Star* details her being gang-raped in high school and sexually assaulted as an adult. "It's like using a bunch of shark attack victims as our lifeguards."

In two recent novels by women, the identity of those shark victims varies according to generational conceptions of how pornography does its damage. Margaret Atwood's novel *Oryx and Crake* offers a "traditional" portrait of abuse. Porn has supplanted intimacy in the novel's devastated near-future setting. "Executions were its tragedies," Atwood writes of this world, "pornography was its romance." Oryx, first sighted by her would-be lover on a kiddie-porn site, is abused starting at a young age, and her eerily flat recounting of the experience is definitely a cliché that bears repeating. "Whatever it was, you had to do it, and you did it because you were afraid not to. You did what they told you to do to the men who came, and then sometimes those men did things to you. That was movies," she concludes.

"It wasn't real sex, was it?" her friend asks, clinging to the illusion that maybe no harm is done during these encounters. "It was only acting, wasn't it?" To this, Oryx replies: "But Jimmy, you should know. All sex is real."

British novelist Helen Walsh's debut *Brass* posits a complex new kind of victim. Millie O'Reilley is a bright but jaded Liverpool college student whose impulses are those of a "female chauvinist pig." For the opening scene alone, where Millie pays for brutal lesbian sex with a teen prostitute in a graveyard, the novel would be a scandal. This young woman, raised by a college professor father in the 1990s, is no more sensitive than the most brutish male. "I manipulate myself hard and selfishly," she says of the encounter, "the whore becoming nothing but a body. A cunt in a magazine." Millie admits that she, too, sees females as objects rather than as humans; she sees them "through the eyes of a pornographer." Though Walsh, who is just twenty-seven, isn't explicit, her character is offered as both victimizer and victim – a distinctly twenty-first-century casualty of porn.

In the eyes of some, Martin Amis's *Yellow Dog* is itself a pornified cultural product. The novel is a calculated howl, and its narrative strategies – various parallel forays into the vast dark cave of what its author elsewhere dubs "the infinite chaos of human desire" – are a challenge. But Amis's point is as clear as his methods are occasionally murky. Men, the novel suggests, have no small amount of trouble maintaining sexual balance in their heads and hearts. The mainstreaming of porn is proving a disaster for this equilibrium, rendering "yellow dogs" out of many males and victims out of many women and children.

Mercifully, it is still men's thoughts, more than their actions, which stumble about in the cave. A father who has suffered a "de-enlightenment" due to an assault starts to fantasize about his daughters.

("They're mine, and I can't protect them. So why not rend them? Why not rape them?") A footman to a monarch is turned on by a movie depicting the deflowering of an actress dressed like the pubescent princess. ("Brendan attended to the ordeal of his own arousal.") A scurrilous journalist wonders about his failures at relationships. ("Each night, as he entered the Borgesian metropolis of electronic pornography – with its infinities, its immortalities – Clint was, in a sense, travelling towards women. But he was also travelling away from them.") Imagine what would happen, *Yellow Dog* contends, if such thoughts were let loose as actual acts committed upon actual people. "We get over it," a porn actress says of the abuse she suffered in childhood. "No you don't," someone else corrects. "No we don't," she concedes. "Obviously."

There is no end to the obvious damage on parade in extreme pornography, should one wish to acknowledge it. Nor is that extremity difficult to find, thanks largely to the Internet. But even if one grants that a pornographic sensibility has gained a degree of mainstream acceptance in society, is there actual evidence of a slippery slope of collective harm? When the Supreme Court of Canada recently ruled in favour of legalizing sex clubs, it declared that there was no sign that "the sexual conduct at issue harmed individuals or society." Dissenters to the ruling, including the editorial writers of *The Globe and Mail*, argued back that the courts should be used to discourage activities that "offend community standards." The paper also decided that waiting until there is a clear indication that indecency is sliding into depravity is waiting, in effect, until too late.

But a consensus about "community standards" may no longer be available. Sex remains a moral issue for most adults, but not in the way it once was. The movement has been away from the morality of sex itself – no pre-marital sex, the proscription of homosexuality – to the issue of harm: people shouldn't be getting off on the acts of those who are themselves traumatized and are being traumatized by what they are doing. Maybe terms like "obscene" and "pornographic" have lost their nuance. Words such as "dangerous" and "humanly disastrous" might be more to the point.

In an essay about the porn industry in California, Martin Amis wrote that "porno is littered – porno is heaped – with the deaths of feelings." To be more specific, in its exploitation of personal tragedy and naiveté, its misrepresentation of human erotica, especially among newly sexualized youths, who may never recover from being consumers of its distortions, in its indifference to consequence, to the casualty of action and effect, both on screen and in real life, extreme pornography may be stalking one emotion more than any other. That would be the shared feelings we have for fellow humans, along with the inclination to recognize kindred suffering and even lend aid. Porn may yet be the death of empathy.

2006

THE BONFIRE IS OUT:

Tom Wolfe In Bush's America

Jojo Johanssen is an all-American kid. One of the college students in Tom Wolfe's new novel, *I Am Charlotte Simmons*, Jojo plays hoops for Dupont, a fictional Ivy League school with the top basketball team in the nation. At six-foot ten-inches, and 250 pounds, he has decent height. He is also bulked up through the biceps and triceps, his shoulders swollen with trapezius muscles the size of cantaloupes. No blushing giant, Jojo wears gear designed to show off those "traps, lats, delts, pecs, abs, and obliques in glossy high definition." Though not ripped like some of the black players – they boast "chocolate brown skin bulged with muscle on top of muscle" – he's still pretty buff.

Adam Gellin, a bright senior at Dupont, knows he won't ever be a sports god. He can't even match the statue of Saint Christopher in the college square. "What bulging delts!" Adam thinks of the saint's granite form. But he can make fun of the "diesels" at the gym. Diesels are non-athlete students who lift weights purely for effect. "The new male body fashion," he sneers to himself, "the jacked, ripped, buff look." Still, the boy winds up sneaking peaks in the gym mirrors in the hope that his own trapezii might be on the rise.

Undergrads, of course, are notoriously preoccupied with sex and booze, self-image and self-discovery. A rollicking satire of college culture delivered in roaring Tom Wolfe prose is bound to be swollen from all the "burgeoning biceps" and "loamy loins," the "grinding groins" of frat-party dancing. The bulge comes with the territory; it is the lay, so to speak, of the fictional land.

Open Wolfe's 1998 novel, *A Man in Full*, though, and find this page-one description of a sixty-year-old Atlanta property developer: "For good measure, he flexed and fanned out the biggest muscles of his back, the latissimi dorsi, in a Charlie Croker version of a peacock or a turkey preening." A former football star, Croker is still impressive and intimidating, even with a bum knee. But then, so are the Bronx district attorneys in Wolfe's 1987 *The Bonfire of the Vanities*. "Andriutti liked the fact that when he reached around behind one of his mighty arms with the other hand, it made the widest muscles of his back, the lats, the latissima dorsae, fan out until they practically split his shirt, and his pectorals hardened into a couple of mountains of pure muscles." Ask Andriutti and his colleagues the names of the planets and they'll shrug. Ask them to pinpoint a deltoid or pectoralis major and they'll draw you an anatomy chart.

I *Am Charlotte Simmons* offers declensions of a dialect Wolfe dubs "college Creole." Selections include "Fuck Patois" and "Shit Patois." "Jacked Patois" is not explored as fully in the novel, but it could be. To "jack-up" literally means to hoist or boost. In American speech, the term is now applied to anything propelled high and far, anything huge and powerful. It works as an adjective ("That guy is jacked"), with or without an exclamation mark ("This whole country is jacked!"), a verb ("Wolfe has really jacked his satire this time"), or even with gentle irony ("He sure looks jacked in that white suit"). The word is a good one, youthful and masculine, suggestive of incisive action and piston-like vigour.

It is certainly a Tom Wolfe word, applicable equally to his sprawling novels and the muscled America they so fondly satirize and instinctively protect. And who can blame a guy, or a nation, for wanting to stay jacked? Steroids or Viagra, Clinton's White House sexcapades or Bush's bench-presses: No one likes turning soft. No one likes growing old.

Few pursuits are given more artistic rope than the great American novel. Two assumptions underpin the tolerance. The first is that the pursuit is a largely male obsession, like whale hunting, and thus is obliged almost by fate to wind up a deforming pathology, the way it did for Melville's Ahab. The second is that the chase, however maniacal, is righteous, given the behemoth-in-question. Even an observer as wry as Martin Amis grants the hunt its nobility. "Every ambitious American novelist is genuinely trying to write a novel called USA," he writes in his 1986 essay collection *The Moronic Inferno: And Other Visits to America*. Amis is referring to the eponymous John Dos Passos epic from the 1930s, a genre benchmark. Such strivings are the "inescapable response to America," and if books tend to be big, it is because the USA is big too.

Tom Wolfe took up his fictional harpoon late in the season. He was approaching sixty when *The Bonfire of the Vanities* appeared, having devoted himself until then to the New Journalism, a school of nonfiction he helped establish and which, in the opinion of many, produced the best American literature of the latter half of the twentieth century. (Capote's *In Cold Blood*, Mailer's *The Executioner's Song*, and Wolfe's own *The Electric Kool-Aid Acid Test* are examples.) He embarked on the novel hunt with the fanfare expected of the man in spats. Less well known is that Wolfe gained literary credentials early on, with a Ph.D. from Yale and a dissertation on communist tendencies among American writers between the world wars.

In a *Harper's* essay published shortly after *Bonfire*, Wolfe declared the American novel a "weak, pale, tabescent" creature in the clutches of anorexia. To revive it would require authors willing to take on this "wild, bizarre, unpredictable, Hog-stomping Baroque country of ours." It would require books pumped up on reportage that met the standard of the New Journalism, and were ready to wrestle with issues such as class, race, and status envy; the very same issues, it so happened, being wrestled in the Hog-stomping work of that journalism's most celebrated advocate. The American novel needed Tom Wolfe, in short, and, lucky for it, Mr. Wolfe was available.

By then, he had won certain bragging rights. *The Bonfire of the Vanities* was not only chubby and apple-cheeked but passionately engaged with its age. Like Upton Sinclair's Chicago or John Steinbeck's California, Wolfe's New York was a literary landscape bristling with social conflict and consequence. The pages swarmed with characters at the mercy of flaws in equal parts worrisome and compelling. The tilt towards excess, the blind faith in a certain version of progress, the hollowness at the centre of the American enterprise: such anxieties simmered at surface level in the book, like tar on hot pavement. The nation portrayed in *Bonfire*, while indeed wild, bizarre, and unpredictable, was equally restless and vital, alive to its own ongoing evolution. It was also naturally outsized, with no need for any Bronx lawyer to flex his pectorals as proof.

But that was before the Berlin Wall came down and the doors shut on the Cold War. History, as Francis Fukuyama announced at the outset of the 1990s, had ended. A happy ending it was, too, with liberal democracy so certain to spread across the globe under the aegis of the U.S. American exceptionalism, a view of the planet from high up in that proverbial city on the hill, reigned triumphant, and the impending New American Century promised even better times ahead.

A satirist of the calibre of Tom Wolfe might have been expected to dress this insularity down, chide it as myopic. Instead, 1998's *A Man in Full*, overplaying its Southern charm and stuffed with the sorts of prolix descriptions of cars and clothes, houses and buildings that so irk Wolfe's detractors, was sleepy and provincial, a retreat from those scalding New York sidewalks. Nor did the book's bulk – 744 cramped pages in the original edition – feel like an inescapable response to America. It felt more like padding or even armour.

Hooking Up, a selection of the author's non-fiction published in 2000, marked a telling interlude between novels. Many of the essays were shameless hymns to the republic. In the title piece we were told that America is now "the mightiest power on the earth" and had "shown the world the way in every area save one" (the area being the arts, which Wolfe found still slavishly obedient to Europe). Elsewhere, he recalled how earlier in the twentieth century his native land had the "glow of a young giant: brave, robust, innocent, and unsophisticated," a glow its leftist writers strove to dull. Writers today were likewise chided for failing to engage with "the rich material of an amazing country at a fabulous moment in history."

"Did a single solitary savant note that the First American Century had just come to an end and the Second American Century had begun?" Wolfe asked in a piece occasioned by the millennium, " . . . and that there might well be five, six, eight more to come? – resulting in a Pax Americana lasting a thousand years?" Dubbing critics of American triumphalism as "Rococo Marxists," he gleefully asserted just how triumphant, and exceptional, was his homeland.

All of which raises a question: Why was Tom Wolfe now metaphorically jacking his nation? America is hardly starved for boosters. Jingoism already rolls off the lips of plenty of its politicians. A novelist can be many things, including a patriot and supporter of George W.

Bush. What he can't be is content to view his raw material – in Wolfe's case, American society in his own lifetime – complacently. If he does, he risks losing more than touch. He risks losing his independence.

Reading Tom Wolfe's novels in sequence is akin to riding a stationary bicycle when you had hoped to be out on the open road. You enjoy the pedalling enough, but not getting anywhere eventually starts to rankle. All those stationary hours naturally turn the mind towards the person putting you through such exercise. Author photographs, spaced over the seventeen-year period between *Bonfire* and *I Am Charlotte Simmons*, reveal more than the advance of an amiable-looking gentleman from his middle years into the golden ones. (Wolfe is now seventy-three.) The photos chart the famous white suit as well. The suit is Wolfe's signature, the emblem of his distinctive brand of cool. He has worn it on every book jacket, and in just about every media photograph, for the past four decades. For large swaths of a remarkable career, he has worn it well.

Parsing the suit while pedalling through 2,036 pages of fiction can help pass an otherwise long ride. In the original paperback edition of *The Bonfire of the Vanities*, Wolfe is dressed for the satirical kill in a double-breasted number, cut with wide lapels and a high-collared shirt. The apparel fits a novel about vanity right down to the embroidered pocket square. Given that social satire leans on exaggeration and grotesquery for effect, you wouldn't want him to come across as any less preening.

For *A Man in Full*, he sports the same suit with a dark blue tie and a jauntily perched white hat. Though consistent with the novel's Georgia setting, the photo seems a bit overdressed, as if the author is costumed like one of the vainglorious characters he intends to skew.

By the time you reach *I Am Charlotte Simmons*, having glanced at the eye-popping Tom-Wolfe-in-a-white-tuxedo-and-black-spats shot used in *Hooking Up*, you are desperate for a wardrobe change. A novel set on a college campus at the turn of the twenty-first century, with so much altered in both America and the world – 9/11 to be exact, and the subsequent war in Iraq – couldn't possibly be attired identically to one set in early 1980s New York. But there is Wolfe in the very same suit and shirt, tie and pocket square – minus, mercifully, the hat.

This doesn't seem right. Time has passed. History has kept on unfolding. As you move through the funny and often entertaining *I Am Charlotte Simmons*, admiring its insights into college sports culture and dazzling ear for American speech, you begin to mull over two concerns. One is familiar: why another buffed, ripped narrative? The other is new: in exactly what country is this story taking place?

Charlotte Simmons is the least pumped and most affecting protagonist Tom Wolfe has created. She is, rather, for the first fifty or so pages of the book that bears her name. A waif from the Blue Ridge Mountains of North Carolina, Charlotte starts out being everything those around her at Dupont College are not: demure and studious, polite and deferential. Early scenes showing the teenager in her backwoods habitat are charming. "I can remember when you was no more'n thhhhhis high," a cousin drawls at her graduation party, "and, shoot, you could talk circles around everybody way back thhhhhhen!"

Soon enough, however, the girl is being tied to the railway tracks of depraved America, where she must weep and wriggle seductively to be rescued. The deflation of Charlotte into a silent-movie heroine robs her of any chance to develop as the singular young woman of those early chapters. Wolfe's fondness for the broad strokes of pulp entertainments – in *Bonfire* an adulterous couple face mob justice for their fornication and sloppy driving; in *A Man in Full* the mere hint of a black-on-white rape threatens to burn down Atlanta (again) – reaches its zenith, or nadir, in *I Am Charlotte Simmons*. The sacrificial-virgin storyline unfolds with an ardour that may prove too much for the sexually squeamish or easily bored.

Such are the materials of the populist. While these plots offer a sturdy framework on which to hang a social critique, the majority of satiric novelists today, including Martin Amis himself, prefer to construct more singular narrative edifices. Their exhaustive reporting and status details notwithstanding, the novels of Tom Wolfe are morality tales in the spirit, and perhaps from the age, of Theodore Dreiser and John Steinbeck. Their trajectories can be captured in blaring headlines and summarized from bar stools.

Part of what Wolfe wishes to expound upon in his new novel is the lingering perfidy of Bill Clinton. *I Am Charlotte Simmons* opens with an aspiring presidential candidate being serviced by an undergraduate.

Illicit oral sex sets the tale in motion, a decent if obvious news hook –
assuming, that is, the book had been published in 2000 or spring 2001.
But Wolfe worked on the manuscript for another two years, during
which time he might have found a more compelling peg on which to
hang his white hat, especially given where he lives: in Manhattan, a
few miles from Ground Zero. The Second American Century, after all,
failed to sweep in as foreseen. September 11 and its fallout appeared to
many a new bonfire worth contemplating.

Page 79 of *I Am Charlotte Simmons* contains the only hint that the
story is occurring in the wake of 9/11. Bemoaning French attitudes
toward the U.S., a character snaps: "They were majorly boring, the
French." The allusion is so fleeting it resembles an anachronism, like a
reference to the attack on Pearl Harbour in a novel set in summer 1941.
In interviews, Wolfe has defended his decision: "I found on campuses
the reaction to 9/11 was zero," he told a British newspaper. "For most
kids, it was just something that happened on TV."

To be charitable, Wolfe may be confusing what young adults
would express to each other, or to the journalist-novelist interviewing
them, with the unspoken concerns filling their heads. To be less kind,
he may be wiping their political minds clear so they can carry on with
what he has already resolved are the preoccupations of college kids
today: sex, beer and social anxiety. The book is adrift in an ahistorical
sea, the better to spare it having to confront what is actually happening
back on the shores of America. Its satire could scarcely be less ambitious, disappointing from an author once admired for hunting only the
biggest whales in the ocean. It is also parochial, containing no foreign
characters or settings, an insularity shared by *A Man in Full*.

And all that bulk? Since *The Bonfire of the Vanities*, there has no longer been a correlation in Wolfe's work between novel size and capturing Baroque America. The opposite may even be the case. Large
chunks of his prose are analogous to the vanity musculature of those
diesels in the Dupont gym. As always with the "bodybuilt," it is hard
to be sure if the jacking is for strength and power or to keep others at a
distance and hold a wavering self-image intact. Or perhaps Tom
Wolfe's novels now function like actual gym mirrors, which, if they are
truly patriotic, reflect back only hugeness and potency, a youthfulness
neither time nor experience can touch.

Maybe that is unkind. But Wolfe now seems too invested in a mythic America to examine the society with the sweep and ferocity that he did just three books ago. Consequently, he can only write the fictions necessary for his politics and, indirectly, his president, ones designed to uphold cherished notions of the country as that city on the hill, astounding and outrageous, aloof from the judgments of those of normal dimensions and appetites living far below.

More than a century ago, another author with a satiric eye and verbal flare, along with a fondness for cream-coloured suits, did write the great American novel. It told the story of a white boy and a black man riding on a river, and its tone is one of elegant, mature reserve. Editions of *Adventures of Huckleberry Finn* run at about 320 pages, and within those confines Mark Twain managed to relay what is both eternal and fluid, dark and light, about his evolving nation. "It was wonderful to find America," Twain once wrote. "But it would have been more wonderful to miss it."

2005

THE DISAPPOINTMENT ARTISTS:

American Fiction In The New Millennium

Felonies!® are dark-chocolate cakes made by the Mister Squishy Company. A new product, the cake is still in the testing phase. Everything from the name, meant to "connote and to parody the modern health-conscious consumer's sense of vice/indulgence/transgression/sin vis-à-vis the consumption of a high-calorie corporate snack," to the packaging, featuring the Mister Squishy icon behind bars with his "eyes and mouth rounded in cartoon alarm," is open to discussion and improvement. Gathered in a conference room on the nineteenth floor of an office tower is a focus group made up of members of the target market for *Felonies!* – males between eighteen and thirty-nine, the "single most prized and fictile demographic in high-end marketing." A pyramid of cakes adorns the table. A facilitator stands ready with a whiteboard and dry-erase markers.

"Mister Squishy" opens David Foster Wallace's story collection *Oblivion*. At some 20,000 words, the majority of them arranged in the looping sentences for which Foster Wallace is renowned, this critique of the "great grinding US marketing machine" is a purposeful slog. On page after page, many without paragraph breaks, the mechanics of that machine, from the pseudo-scientific language to the banal aspirations and practices, are detailed with malicious precision. Riffs on matters ranging from the "high-lecithin frosting" (which must be injected into the cake's hollow by using a high-pressure confectionery needle) to models for market testing (the "anovas" or "ANalysis Of VAriance model, a hypergeometric multiple regression technique") lend the sprawling story a feeling of claustrophobia and, eventually, diminishment. In a world where desires and vices exist to be manipulated and humans are encouraged to think of themselves in strictly economic terms, there is much sustenance but little nourishment.

Terry Schmidt, the thirty-four-year-old focus-group facilitator, is certainly starved. Clinging to the belief that he has "a vivid and complex inner life," Schmidt aspires to extricate himself from these consumer self-conceptions. He is stymied by two doubts. The first is his sense that he has "very nearly nothing left anymore of the delusion that he differed from the great herd of the common run of men." The second follows whenever he looks in the mirror. "So that when he thought of himself now it was as something he called 'Mister Squishy,' and his own face and the plump and wholly innocuous icon's face tended to bleed in his mind into one face, crude and line-drawn and clever in a small way." The dissolving complete, Terry's individuality is doomed. To fill that hole now, he would almost have to eat himself – and that still might not be nutrition enough.

From Melville's benchmark exegesis on whaling to John Dos Passos's urban throngs to Cormac McCarthy's epic delineations of physical violence, the intricate detailing of experience has long been the business of major American fiction. What critic Mark Kingwell calls the "American gigantic" produces its equally outsized literary simulacra, and in the structures of the greatest novels and the headlong momentum of the best prose, the nation is perpetually depicted as an unwieldy, messianic, and decidedly material project. In 1961, Philip Roth admitted that the grandeur and lunacy of the project was "a kind of embarrassment to one's own meager imagination." Embarrassed or not, Roth, Saul Bellow, William Gaddis, Thomas Pynchon, and Don DeLillo, among others, have all published books that match that sprawling reality, if only in terms of aspiration.

Post-World War II materialism carried with it promises of pleasure and freedom, along with a new kind of self-reliance and even self-invention – two further hallmarks of American literary thought. Choosing and buying things made you who you were. But several decades on, an infinitely greater variety of products and pop-cultural distractions are staking claims on that self, using ever more sophisticated information-age marketing. Commodities no longer add up to anything meaningful or helpful to better living; they are now just a disorienting 24-7 barrage of sales pitches and heaps of largely useless stuff. Individuals, especially those who sought to ground their own identities in things, might well be feeling abandoned or simply lost.

Foster Wallace sets his tale of consumerist oblivion in 1995. The decade saw the emergence of a group of novelists, including Rick Moody, Jonathan Franzen, and Jonathan Lethem, who were openly ambitious about reinvigorating the kind of social novel championed by Philip Roth. And yet, almost in advance of carrying this national literary project into the twenty-first century, the younger crowd was suffering pre-emptive insecurities. In a 1996 essay in *Harper's*, Franzen worried that America had become a "tyranny of the literal." Any efforts at satirizing it might end up "bloated with issues" and lacking the space to deal with complexities of character. "Where to find the energy to engage with a culture in crisis when the crisis consists in the impossibility of engaging with the culture?" Franzen asked.

The same year, Foster Wallace admitted to similar qualms. While maintaining that "the texture of the world I live in" was pure pop, with its hyperkinetic pacing and countless distractions, Foster Wallace, then the recent author of *Infinite Jest*, wondered about all the "arch, meta, ironic, pomo" manias of his generation. "I get the feeling that a lot of us privileged Americans, as we enter our early thirties, have to find a way to put away childish things and confront stuff about spirituality and values," he said in an interview. He spoke as well of an "American type of sadness" borne, in effect, from having too much.

Now, a full ten years further along, with these writers into their forties and their nation altered by the shock of 9/11 and the ongoing ravaging of national self-conception from the disaster in Iraq, what has become of such impulses? With one exception, the spiritual, values-driven "stuff" that Foster Wallace alluded to remains unexamined. Meanwhile, pure pop textures rooted in artificial commodities continue to overwhelm books, as though their authors can no longer see any way beyond the dense forest of things.

Jonathan Franzen's *The Corrections*, published in 2001, is a clarion call to put away, or at least put in perspective, manias induced by consumerism. The novel is so alert to the pressures of the dark moment, and so acute in its diagnosis of that shading, that its story of a middle-middle-class America family shines authentic light upon the condition. This may not be immediately evident. At over 500 pages, the book has the requisite bulk, the weight of materialism packed between its covers.

But *The Corrections* displays a thematic concision the rival of Joseph Heller's *Catch-22*. Here, too, the title is the message; various urgent "corrections" are required. Literally, it is the habits of the Lambert family – the secrets and hurts, the addictions and dysfunctions – that require corrective measures. As explored in nearly every paragraph, it is American excess that must ultimately be addressed.

"The Correction, when it finally came," Franzen writes, "was not an overnight bursting of a bubble but a much more gentle letdown, a year-long leakage of value." Though he is talking about the dot-com market crash, he is really describing the newly liberated Enid Lambert. "She was seventy-five," the novel ends, "and she was going to make some changes in her life."

To have plunged into the crisis he outlined in his *Harper's* essay and still surface with a call for transformation is an achievement of both creative thought and conscious determination to not allow himself to be smothered in stuff. That said, Jonathan Franzen's new memoir, *The Discomfort Zone*, is a nearly Russian exercise in nostalgia for vanished lightness, be it early *Peanuts* comics or growing up in a 1960s suburban neighbourhood "cocooned in cocoons that were themselves cocooned." The memoir's tone makes plain that far more warm blood of sentiment and even sentimentality runs through Franzen's veins than the analytical Foster Wallace would ever countenance in print. *The Corrections* may have found it easier to chart a path through the forest only because it declined for temperamental reasons to negotiate its recessed heart.

Rick Moody, in contrast, is a fellow traveller through these nether regions. His latest novel, *The Diviners*, carries the 1990s torch for those arch, meta, ironic, pomo critiques of America. A roaring satire of the entertainment industry circa autumn 2000, the story revolves around a Manhattan production company pitching a miniseries devised as a lark by a dissolute B-movie action hero. The more ridiculous the project becomes – at one stage the treatment promises a cast of thousands, including Attila the Hun and a gypsy diviner named Babu, along with historical locations ranging from ancient Mongolia to West Africa during the slave trade – the more it balloons into a Next Big Thing property. Concurrent with the buzz about this nonexistent banality is an actual television series of equal silliness. Titled *The Werewolves of*

Fairfield County, it tells of humans mutating into wolves in Connecticut. "Into this door, America goes," Moody writes of an amusement park ride, "and pays for its ticket, and from this one America emerges, wobbly in the knees – if it still has knees."

The Diviners teems with funny lively characters, and their careful diversity, from a tyrannical Latino producer to a demented African-American artist, a vacuous white chick named Madison McDowell to a TV shaman called Ranjeet Singh, makes for solid dramatic fiction. But such literal colourization can't overcome the reality that, as with most visual extravaganzas, all the parts are ultimately bit and all the actors are extras. By the end, dalliances with interiority or character development have long been given over to the whammy factor. It is late in the cinema spectacle hour; audiences are expecting stuff to blow up real good.

Not wishing to let anyone down, Moody literally abandons his story to a rant about a stolen presidential election and a corrupt justice system. He has succumbed to such side-bar obsessions before. *The Diviners* devotes chunks of its 567 pages to distended riffs on donuts, bowling, trepanation, divination, tattoos, and dowsing – to mention just a few. The final rant, dubbed "Epilogue and Scenes from Upcoming Episodes," marks less a climax to the action than the moment when the author decides to quit writing his book. The closing line is both perfect and perfectly futile: "All good stories end with a fireball in the sky."

Rick Moody can't find his way out of material America. At the same time, he can't help but presume that all this stuff must have greater import and eventually add up to meaning, if only he keeps scrutinizing and itemizing every conceivable particular. Unlike Jonathan Franzen, Moody is unable to frame what exactly ails his society. That, or else he is suffering a personalized crisis of anxiety and depression about an America "saturated with artifice." "Her father had an ulcer," one character tells a self-help group, "her brother, everyone ulcerated, that was just part of being an American, you bled internally, you oppressed other countries, outside you looked great."

But are the literary behaviours on display in these books – of obsessing over surfaces, of struggling and mostly failing to unearth larger unities – really just the private pathologies of a doomed generation? Recent essay collections by Foster Wallace and Jonathan Lethem offer frank, largely self-aware demonstrations of the variety of disorders at play. The nine pieces in Lethem's *The Disappointment Artist*, while elegant and spare, amount to a shopping list of material compulsions acquired to accompany emotional upheavals in his own "discomfort zone."

"In the mid-seventies," Jonathan Lethem writes, "I had two friends who were into Marvel Comics. Karl, whose parents were divorced, and Luke, whose parents were among the most stable I knew. My parents were something in between: separated, or separating, sometimes living together and sometimes apart, and each of them with lovers." Later in the piece, mulling over a "nerdish fever for authenticity" acquired before the age of ten, and how he "tended to identify with my parents' taste in things, and with the tastes of my parents' friends," he analyzes an argument with his mother over the superiority of pre-versus-post-Sgt. Pepper Beatles. "I identified with my parents in other, murkier, more emotional ways, of course," Lethem concludes. "Not that those are separable from the cultural stuff."

They seem, in fact, inseparable. Again and again in *The Disappointment Artist*, Lethem writes about the loss and grief caused by his parents' breakup and his mother's subsequent early death by mulling over the music and movies, books and comics, filling various rooms at the time. His path to the non-material is through the material, a route that admirers of his wonderfully pop-packed novel about the same urban terrain, *The Fortress of Solitude*, will recognize.

Likewise, admirers who recall the 400-odd footnotes that served to further blur the jittery lens of *Infinite Jest* will nod in weary recognition at the nervous tics rendering the essays in Foster Wallace's *Consider The Lobster* equally eye-watering. Whether it's a hilarious, never-ending piece on the pornography industry or a mock-pedantic discourse on usage in American speech, Foster Wallace is forever piling observation on observation and adding thoughts to thoughts, a dementia that reaches its apogee with the employment of footnotes to footnotes, laid out on the page using diminishing print sizes. Even his details require detailing and even his distractions are distracted. Readers, harassed by the volume of information, may feel themselves trapped in those dark native woods.

Which might, in the end, be the method behind a sort-of-mad genius. Perhaps the only way these authors can think to demonstrate the difficulty of framing the spiritual state of their union is to produce books that are themselves elusive and exhausting, distracted and defeated. Perhaps the compulsions amply aired in these works are themselves meant to be literary demonstrations of how national beliefs can go bad. Is being a writer, or even an individual, in a society foundering on the rocks of its own beliefs-turned-to-compulsions an exercise in verbose, self-abnegating futility? Already in 1996, Foster Wallace seemed to anticipate this possibility. Mulling over how he and his colleagues had been gutted by a tendency to aestheticize and over-intellectualize truths, he wondered if they needed to learn instead how to *feel* the truths of their lives and times, like their parents did. Without this nourishment, his generation could be doomed to find their own frantic, directionless existences a muddle, even to themselves. "I'm nervous, I'm lonely," he said, "and I can't figure out why."

Canadians of a certain age and background grew up inside the same first-growth consumer forest as David Foster Wallace and Rick Moody. We also now negotiate a similar thicket of heedless, ever-expanding consumerism. Privilege manifests itself uniformly across middle-class North America, right down to the privilege of being pitched too many snack cakes. Yet a question arises: why the apparent gap in our respective interests in, and anxieties about, the ever more hard core material come-ons of our shared continent? A pastry consumed in Washington surely isn't so different from one eaten in Ottawa.

On the Ottawa side, the cake is different if it doesn't occur to you to examine it beyond registering, most likely in passing, whether the product is Vachon (local) or Hostess (south of the border). What Martin Amis said of the English novel – that it is often "250 pages of middle-class ups and downs" – is equally true of its Canadian counterpart. The middlebrow is a place where these sorts of examinations are limited by space and taste equally. The kind of crazed, encompassing visions of the national drama common in American writing sit uneasily with Canadian self-image and literary inclinations. There may even be a link between the impulse to remain oblivious to the textures of material existences north of the forty-ninth parallel and the tendency in

Canadian novels to steer clear of formal crisis. Keep the messiness at bay and you can keep the stories tidy.

For a school of American writers, there is no such easy out. For them, Mister Squishy is more than a cake. For better or worse, it is an aspect of the national project. America was, and still is, a revolutionary idea, one fuelled by the feel-good ethos of boundless progress. Each generation is expected to do better than the previous. Each comfort rung must be stepped over to further ascend the ladder.

But what happens when there are no more rungs, or simply no ladder, in sight; when instead of stirring utopian visions there is the flat business-as-usual drudgery of planting, planting that ugly forest. The country falls into a depression, and writers of the generation most affected by this decline experience analogous intellectual and emotional lows. Worse, because their novels are culturally determined to serve as embodiments of that project, the books become almost obligated to reflect in their chaotic structures and the dispirited rhythms of their prose less the failure of the idea of America than the sad mess of it. Once the criteria for progress go missing amid the clutter, there is only discomfort and disappointment, only junk and the analysis of junk.

2007

EVERYONE KNOWS THIS IS EVERYWHERE:

Noah Richler's Literary Atlas Of Canada

In episode seven of *A Literary Atlas of Canada*, the ten-hour *Ideas* series that aired on CBC, host Noah Richler has a breakdown. The Toronto critic is squeezing in a visit to his therapist in between trips to St. John's and Iqaluit, Quebec's south shore and Vancouver Island. The therapist's name is Dr. Atwood, and she possesses a familiar nasal voice and mischievous wit. "The books were getting heavier and heavier," Richler tells her, "and just pressing down on me." The problem, he explains, is that he has been proceeding on the assumption that there must be a "Canadian creation myth" unifying our literature. Only he has been having trouble identifying it or getting others to agree. "This is a difficult land, Doc," he summarizes. "I just don't know why we don't have a decent myth like the Americans do."

Though she chides him for "complaining in a rather obsessive way," Dr. Atwood hears the patient out. Richler has opened the episode, titled "Where the Truth Lies," in typical manner, trudging across Beechey Island in the Northwest Territories, site of the wooden graves that mark the fate of Sir John Franklin's 1845 expedition in search of the Northwest Passage. With the Franklin expedition, Richler claims, we have the "mother of all Canadian creation myths," both for its hubris and its failure. In his view, such myths – the stories we tell to understand ourselves – almost invariably involve failure and disappointment. He mentions the expulsion of the Acadians and the rebellions of Louis Riel, the mistreatment of soldiers during World War I and the abuse of aboriginals in residential schools. A couple of contemporary versions get tossed in as well: the 2004-2005 hockey lockout and the tale of Roméo Dallaire, the Canadian general who bore witness to the 1994 Rwandan genocide.

As he has during the preceding hours, Richler has wandered the country talking to writers about the role of landscape and place in their work. Until this episode he has grouped the conversations equally by region as by theme, and has used the programs to tease out single ideas. In "Whiskeyjack Blues," authors Lee Maracle, Tomson Highway, and Joseph Boyden discuss everything from the trickster figure to the dangerous streets of pre-flood New Orleans, where Boyden lived, by way of exploring how native storytelling functions. "The Company Town" travels from Fred Stenson and a vanished Hudson's Bay trading post in Alberta across to Buchans, the Newfoundland mining town where Michael Crummey was raised, to elucidate the habits of dependency and the "crippling propensity for monopoly" in Canadian life.

Now, though, Richler is seeking affirmation for an actual thesis, one that also spans, in effect, from sea to shining sea. Not only that, his notion about myths of failure is a self-conscious throwback to the nation-building theses of Margaret Atwood's 1972 book *Survival* and, earlier still, Northrop Frye's concept of the country as a hostile "bush garden." His intention is to link the literary present with past cultural observations. But will the Canada of 2005 agree to be bound by any single narrative?

For a while, Richler's thesis of Canada as "perennial loser," as his therapist describes it, seems to be faring okay. Novelists Rudy Wiebe and Guy Vanderhaeghe mull over the Franklin and Riel myths respectively, while Gil Courtemanche, the Quebec author of *A Sunday at the Pool in Kigali*, a novel about the Rwandan genocide, wonders aloud about the problems of founding a national myth without the reserve of a "cruel and fantastic history." Our loyalty is to values, Courtemanche says, "and values don't make for great novels."

Then the trouble starts. Dr. Atwood herself, who might appear a natural ally in the unified-thesis camp, delivers a cheerfully untarnished-by-history reading of the changing landscape. "Canada may be defined," she says, "as the place where one is free to make up Canada." This, after Richler knocks on Wayne Johnston's door, expecting sympathy from the Newfoundland writer whose 1998 novel, *The Colony of Unrequited Dreams*, traces the intersections of public history and Joey Smallwood's private life. But Johnston is having none of the thesis either, and doesn't mince his words. "I have basically no interest at all in the question of where my books fit into a way of interpreting

Canada," he says. He is certain that there is no coherent history worth trying to interpret. "It is extremely difficult and probably pointless to find a unifying idea or concept or even tradition," Johnston says of the country. Canadian literature, he seems to infer, can only ever be defined in physical terms: who writes it, where he or she lives, what compels their imaginations. All metaphysical conjectures are not only that – conjectural, borderline fantasy – but are also based on the false premise that there can be an all-informing theory about Canada, or anything else.

Richler gets testy with Johnston, calling his thinking "preposterous," and later assures listeners that, as per the guidelines of post-structuralism, we are entitled to ignore an author's stated intentions when interpreting his work. Still, he is taken aback by the objection. Johnston suggests that his own novels contain "anti-ideas." The exchange leaves Richler wondering if Canada might actually be an "anti-nation," one that naturally lacks a single governing idea. But he isn't ready to abandon the search for an overarching unity, and what he proposes instead, as "the one resilient candidate for binding myth," is none other than multiculturalism, a social policy/reality that is fluid and active and suited to a nation "living in the vivid present." The series returns to the notion in its final hour.

Noah Richler's breakdown is tongue-in-cheek, of course, as is his confrontation with Wayne Johnston. Both are done in the service of dramatizing a revelation that appears to have occurred during the year-long making of *A Literary Atlas of Canada*. As such, "Where the Truth Lies" is more than just smart, nervy radio. It is radio attempting to be as sprawling, unresolved, and in the vivid present – as rawly physical, perhaps, instead of pretentiously metaphysical – as the country itself.

A ten-hour radio documentary on any subject can easily come to resemble a cross-country car journey in the company of a crashing bore. Because the bore is driving, he dictates the rules: the routes and rest stops, which CDs get played. *A Literary Atlas of Canada* encourages this kind of analogy. It is a road series, and, as expected, certain stretches of highway are more pleasing than others. The glorious Gaspé route, for instance, versus the Miramichi detours through New

Brunswick; the perpetual postcard linking Banff with Kelowna as opposed to the Kenora to Thunder Bay run.

Happily, Richler is a bracing presence behind the wheel. He can be funny (Ottawa is the "Brasilia of the North"), impolitic ("This could be Africa," he remarks about Inuvik's de facto apartheid), scathing ("Empire and its residue teaches all sorts of bad habits," he says of entitled ascendancy in Toronto), and quirky (the NHL lockout as a myth of failure?). He isn't afraid of detours, allowing writers to perambulate if what they are saying is interesting, and, though overly fond of the Beatles, his taste in music is decent.

Nor is this driver afraid of getting his vehicle scuffed en route. Ambient noises surround most of the conversations, ranging from the bird call inflecting Robert Bringhurst's thoughts on storytelling and the natural world to the squeak of boots over snow during a frigid walk down the "road to nowhere" outside Iqaluit. While these backdrops don't always stay where they belong, the sounds ensure that the landscapes rendered alive in books retain their character on radio.

In short, Richler relishes making radio in weather and is willing to go anywhere in any season in order to situate writers in their elements. He certainly delights in producing radio as far away from the CBC Broadcasting Centre in Toronto as possible without needing a passport. (He does leave the country once, to track down Highway in southern France.) In "The Company Town," a metaphysics is posited to account for the decentralization of the Canadian psyche. We abide a bossy central authority – a Hudson's Bay Company, an Ottawa, a Hogtown – in no small part because we know we can count on sheer geography to diminish that control, render it at most a minor annoyance in our lives. While his ambivalence about, or indeed rejection of, centralized power and expertise might explain Richler's peripatetic tendencies, it soon becomes apparent that the real lure is the simple pleasure of being on the road. Following the contours of a vast and differentiated land, Richler's literary Canada is a highly physical place from the start.

The series, largely a sequence of almost novelistic journeys, is bookended by an argument. "The Virtues of Being Nowhere" opens with a three-part declension of Canada as an evolving noun. According to the parsing, the nation started off being "nowhere," a destination literally off the European map. (For native storytellers, needless to say, it was never anything of the sort.) Jane Urquhart's childhood in the deep Ontario bush is presented as a classic nowhere landscape, and Margaret Atwood, a dominant presence throughout, discusses early immigrant writers like Susanna Moodie. (Atwood also observes, "There isn't really any nowhere. There are only other people who *think* a place is nowhere.") Richler remarks on how the "garrison mentality," outlined decades ago by Frye and Atwood and which posited Canadians as quasi-victims of their own harsh landscape, put a stigma on generations of writers. By the sounds of it, certain authors today, including Urquhart, continue to feel that weight.

Next, Canada is redefined as "nowhere in particular." Richler is thinking about urban centres during the last half of the twentieth century – or their much-maligned suburbs, to be more exact. Toronto writers Barbara Gowdy, Lawrence Hill, and Paul Quarrington gather to muse on "Non-Mills," or Don Mills, the suburb built in the 1950s north of the city around the "wilderness of the ravines," and the site of their upbringings. A conversation with M.G. Vassanji, who relates how South Asians living in Tanzania in the early 1970s were excited by Canada without really knowing much about it – a circumstance he describes in *No New Land* – throws up a separate idea: Canada as "anywhere." But thoughts about Canada from outside give way to the third declension, the "somewhere quite distinct" of the nation as it is unfolding in the early twenty-first century.

Episode ten, "Room Available," is titled after a remark by novelist Yann Martel, who once referred to Canada as a kind of giant hotel. Though Martel himself ruefully contextualizes his comment – he simply meant that the country houses a vast range of people, like a busy hotel – Richler decides the metaphor remains apt. Canada's "sole binding myth" is our ever-burgeoning diversity, a "polyphony of voices" that is altering our literary landscapes for the good. Gone, for sure, is the paradigm of the land as an empty place of menace. Multiculturalism has not only validated a "creed of racial sensitivity" among Canadians, encouraging a belated recognition that aboriginals have always lived in those spaces we presumed desolate and hostile, it has also shown us that nearly every place across the country is habitable and safe. "Iqaluit is the new Seattle," novelist Douglas Coupland jokes of the disappearance of hinterlands.

Most of this final hour is devoted to talking to young Vancouver writers, including Coupland, Zsuzsi Gartner, and Timothy Taylor, about their city's unique profile as gritty urban centre and natural wonderment alike. Richler declares Vancouver the perfect setting for Canadian literature to continue to play out these emerging dynamics: diversity and sensitivity, nature as inhabited and yet still disquieting, a society in perpetual evolution. While this may be true, the two most striking radio moments in "Room Available" occur away from the city and serve to complicate the notion of multiculturalism as current binding myth.

First, there is Robert Bringhurst's trance-like monologue on nature delivered from his cabin in the woods of Quadra Island. The pitch of the poet's voice and the cadences of his elegant thinking are offered in harmony with the forest around him. Equally eloquent is the silence – ten seconds of dead air – that greets a question to Rohinton Mistry about whether Canada has had any impact on his novels. Though he eventually replies, Mistry's hesitation is the better answer. Richler is too smart to edit out the pause, leaving it there, perhaps, as a reminder not to speak too confidently about the certain direction of Canadian literature. Writers are by necessity always lost in some space, and it might well not be the one where they reside. You can be near the future of Vancouver and still be creatively sequestered in the past of nearby primal woods. You can be a model of multicultural literary Canada and still be forever at home – on the page at least – in the Parsi community back in Bombay.

A remark by Barbara Gowdy in "The Virtues of Being Nowhere" highlights a tension in the series. Gowdy, who once published a novel about elephants, comments that being from "Non-Mills" may be a blessing for the author who wants to "float out" into the wide imagined universe. Despite its length, *A Literary Atlas of Canada* has little time for discussions about what literary landscapes are and how they are created and sustained. It is almost purely concerned with literature and public discourse and grounding literary realities and, as a result, isn't especially attentive to the qualities of the books themselves or the writerly process.

Throughout the ten hours, dramatic excerpts are offered from dozens of Canadian novels and stories by way of illustrating the observations of their authors. And yet, none of these readings include descriptions of actual places. They are all descriptions of imagined ones. Douglas Coupland may be from Vancouver, but his fiction isn't. His fiction is from his head. Novels are always novels before they are anything else, including mirrors of reality. There seems to be scant room in Richler's atlas for Canadian books situated outside the country or for stories, such as Yann Martel's *Life of Pi*, that openly declare their topographies to be other than approximations of the real. No poetry is welcome either.

Likewise, Gil Courtemanche's invitation to consider a Canadian geography of values isn't taken up. Martel's closing observation that our sole distinguished cultural attribute might be our creed of tolerance is on a similar tack. What about a possible moral landscape running coast to coast in our literature? Wayne Johnston probably wouldn't like this thesis any better, but for this reviewer, at least, the most obvious quality shared among books by Canadians is a certain value system. (That, and a propensity for linguistic conservatism. Aren't the landscapes in novels made up first and foremost by language?) While Richler's instincts to steer clear of literary theory are sound, at times his focus can be constricting.

The explicit assertion of *A Literary Atlas of Canada* is that books published in our continent-sized country must first be approached through their geographies. This is a simple but original thought. Two of the more haunting interviews in the series involve Gwich'in novelist Robert Arthur Alexie and Montreal writer Gaétan Soucy. To better appreciate the implications of these authors officially sharing a literary flag, I read Soucy's *The Little Girl Who Was Too Fond of Matches* and Alexie's *Porcupines and China Dolls* with a view to thinking of them as part of a single literature.

Besides the quality of the work and the portraits of damaged individuals, the distance between the novels includes – in no particular order – 4,000 kilometres, two languages, and at least one cultural and literary tradition. Alexie is a Tetlit Gwich'in native from Fort McPherson in the Northwest Territories. *Porcupines and China Dolls*, his 2002 debut, howls at the disaster of colonialism in the far North. It draws equally on the western novel and storytelling, mixing scenes of raw realism with explosions from the native dream world. The remote Blue Mountains are its landscape. The only non-aboriginal references are to American TV and cinema. Down south means Alberta and British Columbia; Ottawa, Toronto, or any place further east scarcely exists.

Gaétan Soucy teaches philosophy near Montreal. *The Little Girl Who Was Too Fond of Matches*, first published in 1998, is a parable. Featuring an epigraph by philosopher Ludwig Wittgenstein about pain, the book is a prismatic text concerning two siblings raised in a deprivation tank of weirdness and cruelty. Cultural allegiances lie with European philosophy and the new French novel; no landscape is identified, either by location or time. The novel was a bestseller in Quebec and has been translated into numerous languages and widely published abroad. But its muted resonance in English Canada may suggest that recent rumours of the death of the foundation myth of the two solitudes – a binding story that Richler notably downplays – have been exaggerated.

In exactly which ways can one speak of Alexie and Soucy as both being writers of Canadian literature? Certainly not using the same easy definitions that authors from Berlin or the Black Forest might employ to mark their shared identity as German, nor, arguably, with even the confidence that a novelist from Yunnan province in southern China would affirm his kinship with a poet born in Manchuria.

Canada has always been a physical enormity connected by only the most tenuous of theories or, for that matter, railway lines. Now, with many formerly empty zones being filled in by authors such as Robert Arthur Alexie, the country is, if anything, getting bigger by the minute. No surprise, it is also acting less like a nation-state and more like a singular social, cultural, and political entity. Whether or not the overtired word multiculturalism is the right term to describe the literary manifestations of that entity is debatable, and Richler may find a better word in time for the publication of the series in book form in the spring of 2006.

By rendering that vastness and evolution so visceral, and for insisting on taking literature out on the road, *A Literary Atlas of Canada* is engaging in a new kind of thinking. Credit Noah Richler and the CBC for making bookish radio and for recognizing the cultural work that the twenty-first century requires. Nation building – or anti-nation building, perhaps – just can't be like it was back in the old days.

2005

THE PARADOX OF PARADISE:

Adventures In Waynejohnstonland

For those unfamiliar with it, Waynejohnstonland perches on the far cliff-edge of our literary continent. Though already one of the more extravagantly charted terrains in Canadian literature, much of it remains, of necessity, *terra incognita*. By way of introduction, here are twelve key features of its known, sometimes unknowable, and often contradictory topography. All but a few of the excerpts quoted are from *Baltimore's Mansion*, a manifesto about place nestled within a family memoir.

    1. Waynejohnstonland is vast and sprawling. At the same time, it is small and intimate. Finally, its size is indeterminate. "How big is ———land??" the son asks his father in *Baltimore's Mansion*. Replying first that it is very big indeed, the parent adds, "Almost all of it is empty. No one lives there. No one's ever seen most of it."

    2. It is hostile to human habitation. Survivors of early attempts at settlement, safely back home in their beds, often woke up screaming in the night. Only assurances from spouses that they no longer lived in Waynejohnstonland allowed them to find peace again. Alert to this, the German translators of *The Colony of Unrequited Dreams* initially suggested the title "The Territory of Unrelenting Nightmares." Some of this ambivalence appears related to the weather.

    3. In its "dimensions and variousness," it is more a country than a colony or territory. "What a country we could have been," the father tells his boy. "What a country we were one time."

    4. Living in Waynejohnstonland inclines thoughts and propels stories toward the mythic. The author himself hails from the Avalon Peninsula. In the fifteenth-century saga *Le Morte D'Arthur*, King Arthur crosses over to a different Avalon, saying it will "heal me of my grievous wound." Avalon also conjures the Isle of Apples, "a pagan Garden of Eden." As well, there is the "archetypal topography" of Ferryland,

the town where Wayne Johnston's ancestors were born and where, three centuries earlier, a Catholic colony overseen by Lord Baltimore failed to take root in the barren rock. Johnston's blacksmith grandfather was known as "Ferryland's Hephaestus," in honour of the Greek god of the forge, and as a child Johnston imagined his grandparents "barge-borne by the hooded Queen and her assistant queens" for their crossing into Avalon – into the afterlife.

5. The topography is likewise totemic, often arrestingly physical and anthropomorphic, a character unto itself. Ferryland has a head, ears, and a gaze; the city nearby is notable for its brow. From page one of *The Story of Bobby O'Malley*, published in 1985, to the closing pages of *The Navigator of New York*, published in 2002, settings have almost always been first the small towns and then the sole proper city of the land. Book after book animates the capital with the ardour of a tireless love poet. In one novel, it is compared not to a summer's day, as Shakespeare portrayed the muse of his sonnets, but to constellations of stars, "all with their distinctive patterns of lights," as Johnston describes the various neighbourhoods.

6. Residents of Waynejohnstonland are similarly besotted. The society's defining myth is that "the true king [is] always in exile or in rags while some pretender [holds] the throne." Characters are indeed ragged true royals. They also tend to be misfits and loners, alienated from the mainstream and inclined toward private obsessions. Secrets abound, generally concerning parentage. Romances are brief and unsatisfactory. With their extravagant plot twists and old-fashioned interests in fortune and destiny, Wayne Johnston's books share more in common with the tales of Daniel Defoe than with those of Douglas Coupland. "It was the stuff of boys' adventure books," explains the child in *The Navigator of New York*.

7. The land requires keepers for its lighthouse. It scarcely matters whether the applicants are fictional creations, like Sheilagh Fielding in *The Colony of Unrequited Dreams* and now *The Custodian of Paradise*; real people rendered fictional, such as Joey Smallwood in the same books; or even real people rendered non-fictional characters, including the Johnston clan of *Baltimore's Mansion*. The requirements are the same: tenacity, belief, and an appetite for lost causes.

8. Once you leave Waynejohnstonland, you stop believing it is real. Johnston writes of his relatives: "Home, when they left it, had ceased to exist." Not surprisingly, you can't go back either. The author has been in deep, possibly dispiriting exile for years. He lives in Toronto.

9. Waynejohnstonland is a space of "fancy and conjecture" and of yearning and nostalgia. "The past isn't dead," William Faulkner once wrote. "It isn't even past." All of Johnston's major works, beginning with 1998's *The Colony of Unrequited Dreams*, are set in the pre-present.

10. An obvious point, still worth making: Waynejohnstonland is an island. "An island to someone who has never left it is the world," the writer asserts. Equally paradoxical is his companion remark: "An island to someone who has never seen it does not exist." Both comments argue for the importance of psychogeography over any of the objective physical evidence that might be found – or not found – on maps.

11. A corollary point, somewhat less evident: there are smaller islands surrounding this larger isle, rocky crags of still-greater remoteness and inhospitality. Here is a description in *Baltimore's Mansion*: "beyond the island the headlands of another island, partially obscured by mist." Read as a meditation on literary places, Johnston's memoir asserts the primacy of personal geographies, complete with their own myths, in the slow, steady mapping of a writer's preoccupations. While this theme might not have been obvious when *Baltimore's Mansion* first appeared, poised between the exuberantly public *The Colony of Unrequited Dreams* and the still-exuberant, if somewhat ragged *The Navigator of New York*, Johnston's seventh and most expressive novel, *The Custodian of Paradise*, makes this inward turn apparent.

12. Waynejohnstonland resembles a certain real island – a former British colony, now a Canadian province, off the Atlantic coast – from which the author hails. While tempting to indulge, similarities to Newfoundland are ultimately misleading. If anything, with each succesive book the landscape is looking more and more like a garden few have ever seen and none have ever left.

The Custodian of Paradise opens with a retreat from a large island to a small one. It is the final days of World War II and Sheilagh Fielding, the journalist who nearly elbowed Joey Smallwood off centre stage in *The Colony of Unrequited Dreams*, is determined to quit St. John's. She isn't seeking to flee Newfoundland. Quite the opposite: her ambition is to enter even more deeply into its lonely soul. Pestering an official from the registry office, she explains her needs: "I meant an island on which there had once been a settlement but whose population was now zero, not one that had never been settled."

Such a place is soon found – Loreburn, off the southern coast – and Fielding stuffs two trunks with most of her worldly possessions, as well as thirty bottles of Scotch. To others, she declares the exercise a literary one: she intends to write a book. "I've decided it will just be about one island," she claims. But to herself she admits the truth. "Letters of a sort were what I planned to write on Loreburn." Letters, however, that are likely to be burnt shortly after they are composed, and certainly never sent. "How bereft I was of all that was so precious to other people," she says. She is forty-one, and a mental and physical wreck. Suicide by Scotch seems possible.

Mr. and Mrs. Trunk, as the cases are dubbed, also contain Fielding's journals of many years and the notebooks kept by her son, David, forwarded to her not long before by David's twin sister, Sarah. "I stared hard at the trunks," their owner reports during the crossing, "terrified that the rope or winch would break or the trunks would come loose from the hooks and their contents spill irretrievably into the water." The loss of David's writings would be devastating. Baroque circumstances, whose unfolding fuels the plot of *The Custodian of Paradise*, resulted in Fielding having never met her daughter and having seen her son only once. His death overseas has triggered this crisis.

"From this distance," she notes out on the water, "it resembled a massive rock with a dark green mantle of grass dotted white with gulls." But on sighting the actual settlement, her thoughts turn animistic. "Loreburn," she says, "looked to be in a permanent state of mourning, each family withdrawn to endless solitude behind those boarded windows. The houses were like faces whose eyes and ears had been patched and whose mouths had been taped shut." Another failed colony, it would appear, its dreams likewise unrequited.

Long before the nature of Loreburn is revealed, however, it is evident that *The Custodian of Paradise* is charting distinctive terrain.

There are only a handful of characters and scarcely any incidents. There is also little sense of history unfolding, despite the backdrop of the war. Instead, there are the voluminous letters and documents that Sheilagh reads and writes, often describing events decades in the past, and there is the dream-time of a woman sequestered on an island surrounded by the roaring ocean and reeling birds. Nor is there any raucous boys'-adventure cast to the setting. The atmosphere, rather, is one of quiet allegory. .

Mostly, too, there is Sheilagh Fielding herself. Never before has Johnston so given a book over to a single character. Happily, Fielding remains outsized and outlandish, and her emotional vulnerability both propels and occasionally unsettles the narrative. Her fearsome wit, a cross between Oscar Wilde and Dorothy Parker, has also survived intact. "Behold, the lilies of the Feild," she chides the boys of Bishop Feild School as a teenager. "They do not reap. Neither do they sow. Their fathers do that for them." Or this jibe, delivered in the voice of a human-refuse collector, in one of the "Forgeries" columns that establish her notoriety before her twenty-first birthday: "Not everyone can make it to the top. It wouldn't be the top if they did. The top would be the same as the bottom and then no one could make it to the top. Or the bottom. Or the middle."

Joe Smallwood is back as well, though not with the same purpose. "I have seen that scarecrow of a boy," Fielding's father bellows at her. "That worthless wretch. Skin and bones. A crow's nose. Skulking about like a thief." Aside from cameos in a couple of scenes, Smallwood has little to do except be blamed for having impregnated Sheilagh. That he is not the true father represents a small joke on those who complained about the liberties taken with facts in *The Colony of Unrequited Dreams*; instead of a real person cast as a journalist covering a maritime disaster (the voyages of the SS *Newfoundland* and the *Bellaventure*) that actually occurred when he was a boy, we now have a real person falsely accused of fathering fictional babies (the twins, David and Sarah). More seriously, that Joe Smallwood, the character, would be encouraged, so to speak, to consider having sex with Sheilagh Fielding marks a mischievous rephrasing of a favoured Johnston theme – the need for people to crawl out from what the author once described as "the avalanche of history" with their individuality intact. Board a ship that sailed before your time or be rumoured to father babies born only in fiction: both are assertions that, in a book at least, future premier Joey Smallwood can do whatever he wishes – or rather, whatever his creator wishes for him to do.

As if to press this idea home, *The Custodian of Paradise* raises its flag of individuality in the proverbial genesis of archetypes. Literally: Loreburn is the Garden of Eden, with Sheilagh Fielding cast against type as Eve, managing without – for the present – an Adam for company. Few other parallels with the Biblical tale survive. But what Loreburn, home to wild weather and feral dogs, lacks in tropical fruit and reptiles, it makes up for with restorative calm. Here, finally, Fielding finds a way to bring order to, if not overcome, her grief. "There is nothing in the world but water, a patch of it the size of a pond on which it seems we make no progress," she reflects. Her victory over those bottles of scotch, for instance, which stay unopened, may be small, but it is a triumph nonetheless.

Enter Adam. In the book's climax, Fielding's provider, a protector-figure she has known for decades, but only through letters, joins her on the island. Their union occurs in a ruined church – he is a former priest – and is preceded by a no less haunting letter that outlines a personal creation myth for the relationship. The passage, which lends the novel its title, is worth citing in full. The speaker is "Your Provider," and his delegate is the man he employed to intervene directly in her affairs:

"Neither my delegate nor I could ever think of paradise as a tropical place as described in the Bible or by Milton, especially paradise in the wake of Adam and Eve. No, it was always winter there. My delegate pictured it as an island on which God lived alone in a great house to which he 'hoped' his children would return some day, even as he knew that, because of his own irrevocable edict, they never would. 'The paradox of paradise,' my delegate called this. He imagined God at twilight, looking out the topmost window of his house upon an unblemished tract of snow, soon to light the candle that he placed in the window every night as a guide in case the two he sent away for good came back."

God lives for eternity on this wintry isle, awaiting the return of his "fraternal twins." The Provider dubs God the "hermit of paradise" and, in anger, the "charlatan," given how his fall from grace was fixed from the start. Mostly, though, he is the "custodian of paradise," and in the kind of moment of aesthetic precision granted those authors willing to risk all, including readers, to pursue an idea to its limit, Wayne Johnston achieves a breathtaking compression of image and allusion. "We are all three of us . . . custodians," the Provider declares, "withdrawn from the world to preserve, to keep inviolate, something that would otherwise be lost."

"Many writers," the American author Annie Dillard wrote, "do little else but sit in small rooms recalling the real world." Dillard gets the location right, and her descriptions of the loneliness that accompanies prolonged solitude are apt. But she is wrong about the subject of those sittings. Writers are rarely recalling the real from inside their rooms. Instead, they are perpetually recharting their own imaginative terrains. They are, in effect, creating parallel continents and countries, cities and towns, and are doing so with obstinacy and vigour. These inner geographies float free of, but are also often irreducibly intertwined with, the places where we are born, live, and die.

Always, too, writers behave as the Old Testament God does toward His creations. It is impossible to avoid the implications of Johnston's organizing metaphor. The creative act, especially in narrative form, is uncannily akin to the story of Eden. Writers do fix tales in order that their beloved characters get expelled from one garden or another, and then keep vigil for those characters long afterward. Predictably, the novel is obsessed with the geography of books, and especially with interior landscapes – the ones all humans inhabit, no matter where they actually reside. Is the Garden of Eden not the original literary setting? As an allegorical space, it stands in for our self-awareness as a species, our utopian yearnings, and eternal falls from grace, our compulsive flights from paradise.

That space, intimate and dreamlike, is both the opening and final terrain of *The Custodian of Paradise*. It would be a mistake to view the novel as a sequel to, or even a mirror image of, *The Colony of Unrequited Dreams*. Nor is it safe to assume that the "something" requiring preservation in this latest Wayne Johnston fiction, the thing that might otherwise be lost, is the pre-Confederation Newfoundland portrayed so ardently in his previous books. *The Custodian of Paradise* is a declaration of independence from the tyrannies of external topographies, of public history, and of plot. As such, it is not so much the most ambitious mapping to date of Waynejohnstonland as the first proper excavation of its landscape. In choosing to dig up his own site, to unearth settlements and gardens lodged within the archaeological record, Johnston is going about the business of the major novelist in mid-career: custodianship of his own properties. Asserting that a spit of rock in the Atlantic Ocean is a snowbound Eden is not so strange if your spadework has revealed the layers underneath. Chip away at connections, sift through stories and metaphors, especially of the sort you have been digging away at for years, and conclusions become inevitable, as do perfect truths and perfect paradoxes.

Literary tours of James Joyce's Dublin or William Faulkner's Mississippi aside, it is worth remembering that readers of novels cannot declare with confidence that they are visiting any place other than an author's head. Perhaps, in the end, places really exist only in the imagination. The playfulness of *Baltimore's Mansion* flagged Wayne Johnston as an artist unwilling to be affixed so readily to a map of literary Canada – or, for that matter, of literary Newfoundland. His imagination declines to be bound by that kind of geography. He isn't even certain an island exists if no one has seen it. "Knowing I would lose sight of Newfoundland eventually," he writes of his own leave-taking as a young adult, "I did not stand at the rail. Instead I sat facing away from it for as long as I was able to resist the urge to look. And when finally I did look, it was gone."

2006

WHAT WE WANT FROM NOVELS:

In Praise Of (A Little) Difficulty

On a stop in his hometown of St. Louis during a 2001 book tour, Jonathan Franzen did the following things to try and please a camera. Because his novel *The Corrections* features a character who is a railway man, the author agreed to wander a transportation museum for an hour, looking contemplative. Because the plot builds towards a Christmas family reunion, he taped a scene where he drove across the Mississippi river, acting the prodigal son. Four takes were needed to capture the author turning pensively onto the street where he grew up. Then, when Franzen declined to be filmed outside his family home – his parents had passed away not long before – a half hour was devoted to him walking towards the tree on a traffic island where his father's ashes had been scattered. He was coached for this scene. "You're walking towards the tree," the TV producer told him. "You're thinking about your father."

That same evening, Jonathan Franzen flew to Chicago to record a ninety minute interview for the show the footage would be used on – 'Oprah.' Oprah Winfrey had selected *The Corrections* for her book club, declaring that the author had poured so much into the novel "he must not have a thought left in his head." Her comment proved prophetic. By his own admission, in the following days an exhausted, endlessly-touring Franzen made a series of imprudent comments, including critiquing the Oprah book club logo and employing the term "high art" when discussing his own writing, or at least the writing of those authors, such as Proust, Kafka and Faulkner, who had influenced him. The remarks led Winfrey to uninvite the novelist. In the ensuing media drubbing, the *Boston Globe* dubbed Franzen a "pompous prick" while the *Chicago Tribune* labelled him a "spoilted, whiny little brat."

Imagine, even for a moment, William Faulkner being instructed to wander the streets of Oxford, Mississippi, looking pensive. Or Franz

Kafka fielding requests that he ruminate on the autobiographical elements of *The Castle* with the sun setting over the Prague skyline. Or
Marcel Proust, posed nibbling on madelines in a Paris cafe. "You're
staring at the pastry," the producer would be saying. "You're thinking
about pretty much everything."

Imagine any of these scenes of author genuflections before the
schoolyard mite, and muscle, of the media.

We expect a lot from our novelists these days, especially those who
insist on clinging to the literary tag. And why not? We read a few of
their books in large numbers and award the odd one a prize. We occasionally do some lucky writer a favor by adapting his story for the
movies. For that matter, we throw authors everywhere a bone by reading books at all, given the number of DVDs that require viewing. Then
there is the effort-to-reward ratio. People can listen to a stack of CDs
and watch a miniseries of television and even read a pile of magazines
and other kinds of books, all in less time and with far less strain than is
needed to get through a so-called serious novel. Thus, anyone who
does give a literary fiction a go wants something in return. It's only
natural.

What readers want most, I sometimes think, is less. They want
less novel and, in effect, more author. Or rather, they wish both writer
and book to look and act more like mainstream movies and TV. If
there is a truism about the camera, it's that it appreciates surfaces (the
writer) and struggles with depths (the book). Narrow the gap between the two – say, to a nice middlebrow range – and you've got a
show worth airing. Maintain the distance between creator and creation, or even simply express discomfort at the process, as Jonathan
Franzen did, and you've got a problem. Worse still, you've become
the problem: the problem author and/or the problem book. In current
parlance, you've got an 'elitist' whose work is 'pompous' and 'inac-
cessible.'

I was once invited to be a book club guest. The invitation was a
pleasure, and I spent the evening talking about books with a dozen
passionate readers. It was nice and club members were nice and I was
happy to be there. One of their previous selections had been Michael
Cunningham's *The Hours,* a novel about, in part, the life of Virginia
Woolf. They had loved the book and the film made from it. So much so,

that they had decided to add Woolf's own *Mrs. Dalloway* to their reading list. It was, after all, the manuscript the author is shown working on in *The Hours*.

What a mistake. To a person, the club hated the novel, finding it slow, obscure, and unsatisfying. Their disappointment blurred into a simmering resentment expressed toward Virginia Woolf herself, both for writing such impossible prose and, I began to sense, compromising the feelings of empathy the club members had been nurturing for her – or, at least, for Nicole Kidman's representation of her. I commiserated. But I also attempted to explain why literary modernism had approached language and experience in the ways it did. To no avail: Virginia Woolf had become a problem author with a problem book. In coming to her defence, I, too, wound up revealing the literary snob within.

Modernism is enemy number one right now. In an essay in *Time*, critic Lev Grossman blamed the likes of James Joyce and T.S. Eliot, with their complex works "impossible to understand without (and, arguably, with) compendious footnotes and critical apparatuses," for the rise of literature that is difficult, boring and low on the fun count. He even suggested that modernists have caused Americans to betray their better reading instincts. "As much as Americans like to be democratic in their politics," he wrote, "they have become aristocratic in their aesthetics."

Grossman was certain there was an age where commercial popularity and artistic excellence lived in book bliss. He hauled out, as does nearly everyone who wants to rag on contemporary fiction, the era of Charles Dickens, when literary and populist were supposedly united in matrimony, lovers of roaring plots and outsized characters, endings both happy and just. It is true that Dickens had a wide readership and it is probably true, as Grossman put it, that "no one looked down on Scott and Tennyson and Stowe for being wildly popular."

Equally true, however, is that long before Victorian fiction there was Sterne's *Tristram Shandy* and Swift's *Gulliver's Travels*, canonical works that may or may not be impossible to understand without critical apparatuses. Likewise, in the near immediate wake of Dickens and company there were aspiring modernists such as Oscar Wilde and Joseph Conrad. They posed challenges to readers and critics alike; they could, and still can be, difficult to read. There is a historical pattern to literary fiction, but it isn't the pleasing before/after schism put forth by those with various problem authors on their hit list.

Curiously, the *Time* critic wasn't much impressed with the apparent harmony achieved by the same Jonathan Franzen. *The Corrections* is a luminous novel, heartfelt and stirring and written at a remarkable pitch, and it deserves its many admirers. But Grossman, who recognizes a living problem author as easily as a dead one, slotted Franzen amongst the "brilliant mandarins," predicting *The Corrections* would fade, unlike the works of more plot-oriented – and therefore lovers of democracy? – writers such as Donna Tartt and Alice Sebold.

"Books aren't high or low," Grossman wrote. "They're just good or bad." Anyone who has spent time among New York editors will recognize the mantra, another false dichotomy aimed at the perceived enemies of easy reading. The sentiment is, first of all, a paraphrase of Oscar Wilde: "There is no such thing as a moral or an immoral book. Books are well written, or badly written." What the updated version lacks in wit – elitist, mischievous Wildian wit, no less – it makes up for in fake self-righteousness. Who says a literary novel is 'high' while an Elmore Leonard crime novel is 'low'? They just aren't the same kind of book. They have different intentions and ambitions and should be judged by those measures. There are 'good' and 'bad' literary novels and there are 'good' and 'bad' crime novels. It is, or at least it seems to be, that simple.

Simple, too, are the few hard rules of novel writing. To each original story an original structure. To each new voice a fresh perspective. Leave the form just a little bit different from how you found it. Avoid the opening line: "A shot rang out in the dark."

But then what is one to make of the *New York Times* critic who recently suggested that Toni Morrison and Cormac McCarthy pick up an Elmore Leonard book in order to learn how to write? This sounds like bullying, and it sounds like the complaint of someone who is angry that any writer would still expect a reader – a reader who is doing the scribe a favour in the first instance – to work for her pleasure. Elmore Leonard doesn't make such a demand. Neither do magazines or TV or all but a few art-house films. People are busy these days. They've got plenty of other pleasuring options. And don't forget this simple principle: surfaces please, depths frustrate. Proceed accordingly, literary authors.

For all the current pressures, the novel remains a protean literary form. At its best, it defines, rather than reflects, the era. At its most cocksure, it scarcely worries about what the other arts are up to, even the movies, being so convinced that it has no aesthetic or even entertainment equal. Whatever its actual confidence-level, it sure shouldn't take its marching orders from TV producers or, to be blunt, critics with either attention deficits and/or latent feelings of hostility towards art. The recent publication of Edith Grossman's new translation of *Don Quixote*, a novel of volcanic originality and enduring freshness, is evidence enough that the novel has long placed demands on readers, and long rewarded them for their efforts. More than a little name-calling will be needed to shame or tame this behemoth.

2004

ACKNOWLEDGEMENTS

Some of these essays were originally published, in different form, in the following publications: *Brick, CNQ: Canadian Notes & Queries, Far Eastern Economic Review, The Globe and Mail, Maisonneuve, Queen's Quarterly, The Utne Reader,* and *The Walrus.* An earlier version of 'Join the Revolution, Comrade,' appeared in *To Arrive Where You Are: Literary Journalism from the Banff Centre,* published by Banff Centre Press, 2000. I would like to thank all my editors: Michael Redhill and Esta Spalding at *Brick;* Martin Levin and Jack Kirchhoff at *The Globe and Mail;* Derek Webster at *Maisonneuve;* Boris Castel at *Queen's Quarterly,* Kim Echlin at the Banff Centre, and Sarmishta Subramanian, Daniel Baird, and Ken Alexander at *The Walrus.* Though I have not included work published under their editorship, a collection of essays seems the right place to express my gratitude to John Fraser, Anne Collins, Ken Whyte, and Derek Finkle for their support over the years. I am also grateful to Dan Wells at Biblioasis, and wish to acknowledge the counsel of the following friends: Mark Abley, Bryan Demchinsky, Pico Iyer, Mark Kingwell, and David Manicom.

Finally, I would be remiss if I didn't isolate one editor for special thanks. Ken Alexander is a singular creative force guiding a singular cultural institution. A full half the pieces in this book were born and nurtured in *The Walrus,* and I am a better writer for having had these opportunities to work with Ken and his staff.

Charles Foran is the author of seven books. He lives with his family in Peterborough, Ontario.